Allan Konya

drawings by
Charles Swanepoel

Design Primer
for
Hot
Climates

The Architectural Press Ltd · London

First published in 1980 by
The Architectural Press Ltd: London

© Allan Konya 1980

ISBN 0 85139 140 0

Filmset in 10 on 12 point Times and printed in Great Britain by
BAS Printers Limited, Over Wallop, Hampshire

Design Primer
for
Hot
Climates

Contents

Introduction

> Every continent has its own great spirit of place. Every people is polarised in some particular locality, which is home, the homeland. Different places on the face of the earth have different vital effluence, different vibrations, different chemical exhalation, different polarity with different stars: call it what you like. But the spirit of place is a great reality.
>
> D. H. Lawrence

Man today lives in an age of nationalism and triumphant international technology; these now evolve as if they have escaped from human control and acquired a life of their own. Most nationalities have emerged as a consequence of the efforts of a group of people to achieve cultural identity or social equality, but while national cultures are still being shaped by conscious political design, their evolution is now influenced at least as much by international technology and economic forces as by local cultural ones. The danger, however, is that diversity is being gradually eroded through attempts to achieve cultural uniformity on behalf of an expanding market economy.

The exciting diversity of the world is owed to the fact that each person and each place exhibits uniqueness of characteristics and of fate. People like Lawrence Durrell and René Dubos, for instance, believe very strongly that environment profoundly affects human development; that man in his daily life constantly responds to buildings, landscapes, trees and other elements of the non-human universe as much as he does to social experience. The openness of vast plains or seashores makes the body and mind different from what they would have become in the subdued light of forest clearings or mountain valleys. One may doubt this, but what is certain is that any good building should relate and respond not only to the climate and other environmental conditions in its own area, but also to the traditional way of life of its users. This all seems very obvious but, unfortunately, it is all too often ignored or forgotten.

Man, it seems, has forgotten how to design with nature and tends to ignore the climate while he has become preoccupied with forms currently fashionable. The modern building—office or dwelling—looks much the same the world over because, among other things, it has been designed largely to keep natural phenomena outside, to separate conditions inside from the outdoors as much as possible, relying on mechanical devices and systems to do much of the work.

Architecture and planning know-how cannot simply be exported as if they were some standard consumer product and it is essential for anyone wishing to work abroad (whether in a foreign land or another region of one's own country) to appreciate and understand the unique situation of the area concerned; to have a deep insight into not only the physical elements such as climate, environment, materials readily available, local technology and techniques, but also the political structure, social conditions, religious values and life-styles.

The hot tropical and sub-tropical regions contain most of the world's population and, even in the developed world, it is here that the majority of new buildings will be built. For this reason this book concentrates on these regions but, as no book can give all the information required, let alone a respect for and sensitivity to the 'spirit' of any place, serves only as a broad outline of the climatic, environmental and technological conditions. It is meant not only for designers from temperate climatic areas but also for those who live in these regions, in the hope that they will be stimulated to re-examine conditions which may have become over-familiar to them.

7

Chapter 1

Climate, zones and comfort

Introduction

The climate of a given region, which not only plays a great part in the composition of the soil but also affects the character of plants and animals and the energy of men, has come to be regarded as a description of the prevailing conditions and is determined by the pattern of several elements and their combinations and interactions.

The principal climatic elements, when human comfort and building design are being considered, are solar radiation, temperature, humidity, wind, precipitation and special characteristics such as lightning, earthquakes, dust storms and so on. A certain amount of climatic data for the given location must be collected and analysed: monthly mean maximum and minimum temperatures, the diurnal range, monthly mean maximum and minimum relative humidity values, average monthly rainfall, sky conditions, average amounts of solar radiation, and the direction and velocity of prevailing winds, among other things. The frequency, likely duration and nature of any extreme climatic phenomena must be ascertained, as even though they may be relatively rare and of short duration and, therefore, be acceptable from the point of view of human comfort, they must be considered in order to ensure structural safety.

Buildings in harmony with local climate (Menaa, Algeria). Massive walls and small windows are well suited to very hot days, and cold nights, producing relatively equable internal temperatures

The modifying effects of microclimatic conditions must also be considered. Some knowledge of the character and abundance of vegetation, for example, is also essential because, although it is generally regarded as a function of climate, it can influence the local or microclimate.

Climatic elements

Although a full description of these elements, their distribution, measurements and interaction is beyond the scope of this book, a general description and brief introduction is needed and will be helpful in understanding later sections.

Solar radiation

The three ways in which energy can be transferred from one point to another are radiation, conduction and convection. While transfer of energy by conduction and convection is relatively slow and requires the presence of some intermediate

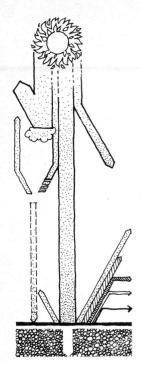

substances, radiation transfer in contrast occurs with the speed of light and can take place without the presence of matter between the radiator and the receptor. Radiation transfers energy by means of electromagnetic waves, leaving an extremely wide range of wave-lengths.

Solar radiation, which occurs in the so-called short wave-lengths, is the source of almost all the earth's energy and is, as a result, the dominating influence on all climatic phenomena. The intensity of solar radiation at the upper limits of the atmosphere varies according to the earth's distance from the sun and the solar activity, but the average intensity on a surface perpendicular to the solar rays is 1.94 cal/cm^2/min (or 1353 watts/m^2) and this value is called the solar constant.

As the radiation passes through the earth's atmosphere a series of losses occurs and the amount of reduction depends on the length of the atmospheric path it must traverse. A part of the incoming solar radiation is reflected by the surface of the clouds, and part is absorbed by atmospheric ingredients such as ozone, water vapour and carbon dioxide, while a certain amount is scattered in all directions by the air molecules themselves. The intensity of the direct radiation depends, ultimately, upon the solar altitude—since that determines how much atmosphere the rays have to traverse—and the amount of water vapour, dust particles, and man-made pollutants which the atmosphere contains. Part of the scattered radiation, called 'diffuse' since it comes from all parts of the sky, reaches the earth's surface and so the total irradiation or insolation (radiant energy received from the sun by the earth) is the sum of this diffused radiation and the direction radiation.

(Above) The passage of radiation through the atmosphere and the heat released from the ground

(Right) In arid zones a large percentage of the radiation reaches the ground (**a**); most of it, however, is lost at night (**b**). In humid zones only around 40% reaches the ground (**c**); about 50% of the earth's heat escapes at night (**d**)

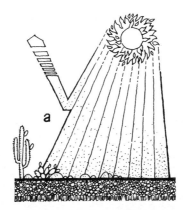

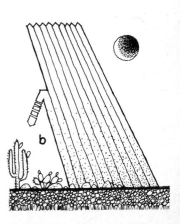

In the annual mean for the whole planet, only about half of the solar energy incident at the outer edge of the atmosphere penetrates as far as the earth's surface, where most of it is absorbed and converted into heat, while the remainder is either reflected back into the atmosphere or used up in the evaporation of water. As the surface of the earth absorbs energy its temperature increases and it, too, radiates energy, though in this case with a long wavelength which can be strongly absorbed by the atmosphere that tends to allow the direct short-wave radiation to pass through without absorbing much of it. As the atmosphere absorbs energy, its own temperature is raised and it, in turn, radiates heat, some downward to the earth and some outward to be lost in space.

Solar radiation varies greatly with the geographic location, the altitude and the weather; in other words with the length of the day, the angle of the sun's rays to the ground, with the length and quality of atmosphere through which it passes, and particularly with the cloud coverage. In general, the greatest amount of radiation is found in two broad bands encircling the earth between 15° and 35° latitude north and south, where, in most areas, the percentage of direct radiation is very high. The zone receiving the second highest amount of radiation, the equatorial belt between 15°N and 15°S, has a high humidity and is frequently cloudy, so the proportion of diffused radiation is high in most of these areas.

The four main channels of radiant heat transfer affecting buildings are, in order of importance: direct short-wave radiation from the sun; diffused short-wave radiation from the sky-vault; short-wave radiation reflected from the surrounding

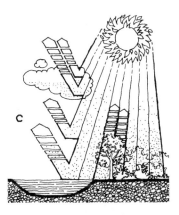
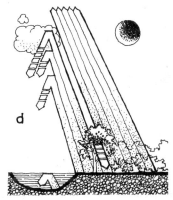

terrain; and long-wave radiation from the heated ground and nearby objects. These affect buildings in two ways: firstly, by entering through windows and being absorbed by internal surfaces, thus causing a heating effect and, secondly, through being absorbed by the outside surfaces of the building creating a heat input, a large proportion of which is conducted through the structure and eventually emitted to the interior. Another major form of heat transfer affecting buildings is the outgoing long-wave radiation exchange from building to sky—an effect which is reduced when the sky is clouded and is strongest when the atmosphere is clear and dry as in hot-arid zones where it can be utilised as a source of energy for cooling buildings.

In the hot climate areas of the world it is particularly important that these effects are influenced (if not determined) by the designer, and how this can be done is discussed in more detail in later sections.

Air temperature

Since air temperature varies from one side of a building to another, from shaded to unshaded areas, from grassed or paved fields to paved roads, it is an element which is difficult to define and in measuring it one can only hope to find a value which represents some average value of the temperature condition of a heterogeneous mixture of air.

The rate of heating and cooling of the surface of the earth is the main factor determining the temperature of the air above it. The air layer in direct contact with the ground is heated by conduction and this heat is transferred in turn to the upper layers mainly by convection and as a result of turbulence and eddies in the air. Since the heating of the lower parts of the atmosphere depends on convection, turbulence and, of course, the acquisition of long-wave energy from the earth, the nature of the ground is important to air temperatures. Soil particles, for instance, enclose a great deal of air which is an effective insulator and, therefore, a relatively thin surface layer of land heats and cools quickly so that in hot deserts the surface temperature may become very high indeed.

At night and during winter the surface of the earth is usually colder than the air as a result of long-wave radiation to the sky, and so the net heat exchange is reversed and air in contact with the ground is cooled. Generally, temperatures are lowest just before sunrise, as diffused radiation from the sky causes temperatures to rise even before dawn, and highest over land

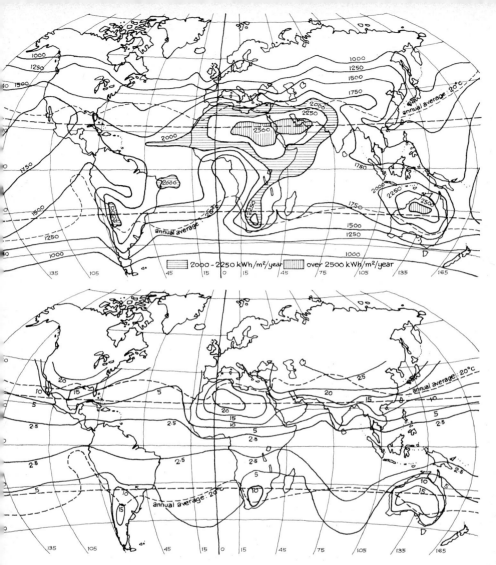

Top) Mean annual solar radiation in kWh/m² per year on a horizontal surface at ground level

Above) Annual temperature range

about two hours after noon, when the effects of the direct solar radiation and the high air temperatures already prevailing are combined.

It is important for the designer to obtain not only the monthly mean maximum temperatures, but also the monthly mean minima, which will give an indication of the diurnal (day and night) variations. These can be large, for instance, in the hot arid zones, and building design must make allowances for this. A large diurnal range is indicative of dry weather and clear skies and the designer can anticipate intensive solar radiation by day and strong outgoing radiation by night pointing, broadly

13

speaking, to the importance of shading, reflective colouring and, possibly, outdoor sleeping. A small diurnal range, on the other hand, indicates overcast skies and a humid climate or season, and points to the need for air movement and protection from rain, among other things.

Wind

Direction, speed, gustiness, and a frequency of calms are all important characteristics of wind, which is a very unstable parameter in most parts of the world, fluctuating markedly within a matter of minutes or hours and changing direction with passing weather systems. The variability of the wind is revealed in both its direction—which always refers to the direction from which the wind is coming—and its speed.

The winds over a region, their distribution and characteristics, are determined by several global and local factors. The principal determinants are the seasonal differences in atmospheric pressure between places, the rotation of the earth, the daily variations in heating and cooling of land and sea, and the topography of the given region and its surroundings.

It would be impossible to discuss here all the causes, or to investigate all the influences which are responsible for the complex and changing atmospheric movements, but it is important to point out that there are types of wind which occur, and recur, in place and time with some regularity. Some of the patterns of air circulation are those which stem from unequal heating at lower and higher latitudes.

Over each hemisphere of the earth's surface there are belts and centres of high and low atmospheric pressure, some of which are permanent while others only exist for part of the year. The main cause of these cells and belts is the uneven distribution of solar radiation over the earth and the resultant variation in surface heating. In each hemisphere the prevailing winds in various latitudes are grouped into three main global belts: the tropical easterlies or trade winds, the mid-latitude westerlies, and the polar winds. There are, in addition, wind systems known as the monsoons which are the result of annual differences in heating of land and sea areas. The mass of air moved by these wind systems brings with it characteristics it has acquired at its place of origin and on its way. On arrival it may replace completely, or mask, more local climatic elements and so come to determine the weather of the whole region. The place of origin of each air mass, and the nature of the surface over

14

which the air moves are therefore significant.

The weather at any place, however, can be affected not only by air moving under the influence of huge air masses, but also by winds of a more local origin which are typical of that area and are caused by a feature of the particular locality such as mountains, a lake or the sea.

Because wind affects ventilation, can be used for cooling, can cause driving rain, can carry dust and can require structures to be strengthened, the designer must determine the direction, speed and predictable daily and seasonal shifts of prevailing winds, and analyse how best to utilise or block the positive and negative aspects.

Atmospheric humidity

The term atmospheric humidity refers to the water vapour content of the atmosphere gained as a result of evaporation from exposed water surfaces and moist ground, and from plant transpiration. For any given temperature there is a limit to the amount of water that can be held as vapour, and the air's capacity increases progressively with its temperature. The vapour distribution is, as a result, not uniform and varies parallel with the pattern of annual solar radiation and temperature average, but is highest in the tropical regions and decreases towards the poles.

Several terms such as absolute humidity, specific humidity, vapour pressure, and relative humidity are used to express the moisture content of the air. Absolute humidity is defined as the weight of moisture in a given volume of air (g/m^3), while specific humidity is the weight of moisture in a given weight of air (g/km). The vapour pressure is that part of the total atmospheric pressure which is solely due to the water vapour, and ranges from a pressure of less than 2 millibars in cold regions and deserts to a pressure of 15–20 (or even more) millibars in hot wet tropical regions.

Although the absolute humidity of a given body of air does not alter unless water vapour is either added to or taken from it, the relative humidity of the air concerned will vary with any change in temperature.

If the air actually contains all the water vapour it can hold it is said to be saturated and its relative humidity is then 100 per cent, but if the actual vapour content is less than the potential content at the same temperature, the relative humidity is then less than 100 per cent. Relative humidity, therefore, is the ratio of the actual humidity in a given volume of air to the maximum moisture capacity at that particular temperature.

As relative humidity affects the behaviour of many building materials and their rate of deterioration, and vapour pressure affects the rate of evaporation from the human body, these two expressions of atmospheric moisture content, both of which vary greatly with the place and time, are most important from the designer's point of view. Whereas the diurnal differences in vapour pressure levels are small, they are subject to wide seasonal variations and are usually higher in summer than in winter. Relative humidity on the other hand may, as the result of the diurnal and annual changes in air temperature which determine the potential moisture capacity, undergo wide variations even when the vapour pressure remains almost constant.

Precipitation

When unsaturated air is cooler, reducing its moisture holding capacity, its relative humidity rises until it eventually becomes saturated and any further cooling leads to condensation. Air may be cooled by coming into contact with cooler surfaces, mixing with cooler air, and by expansion associated with rising air currents. It is only in the lower layers of air that cooling by contact with colder surfaces occurs, and when condensation results it takes the form of dew on the cold surface. When the air not in direct contact with the cold surfaces is cooled below its dew point, fog—a dense layer of droplets lying close to the ground—is formed.

Large-scale cloud formation and precipitation result from what is called 'adiabatic' cooling of large air masses, and are affected greatly by the vertical stability of the air. As air rises the pressure on it decreases and it therefore expands and is cooled; this cooling is known as adiabatic—a change during which no heat energy is gained or lost. When a mass of rising air cools by expansion and reaches its dew point, large-scale condensation occurs, and when countless millions of these droplets, or minute ice crystals are maintained in the atmosphere by upward movements, clouds are formed. As the air continues to rise, the small droplets coalesce into larger and larger drops until they are able to fall by gravity and precipitation—which comes in many different forms such as rain, snow, sleet and hail—occurs.

16

Three major processes resulting in the air currents which, if moist enough, cause precipitation are convective activity, orographic uplift, and convergent (also called frontal or cyclonic) activity. Each of these processes provides distinctive patterns of precipitation. Convective activity, developing from the heating of masses of air in contact with hot surfaces, results in the creation of vertical air currents, clouds and precipitation. Convectional rain usually falls in short but heavy downpours and occurs mainly in tropical regions during the afternoons of the hot season. Orographic precipitation, resulting from air moving upwards over mountain barriers, produces a pattern of heavy rain on the windward side, while the leeward side will be much drier. In this way a mountain ridge may mark a sharp division between quite different climatic types.

Convergent precipitation occurs with the elevation of air—in a swirling or rotational motion—in regions where air masses converge at low pressure zones or fronts. At middle latitude convergent fronts contact is between cold air of polar origins and warm tropical air. The warm air is forced to rise over the colder air mass, usually at a gradual rate of elevation, and the rain resulting from this slow ascent is most often gentle, widespread and of long duration. At the tropical front, on the other hand, the two air streams have similar characteristics and this simultaneous ascent is rapid, usually resulting in torrential rain. Tornadoes, which are small systems of this type with air spiralling at tremendous velocity, form over land in the outer tropics and in the near-tropical regions, mostly when the air is moist and unstable, especially in the hot afternoons. Thunder-

Average annual precipitation

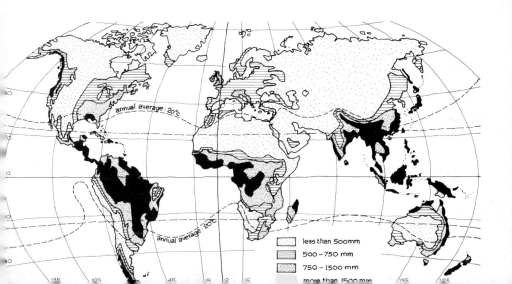

annual average: 20°C

annual average: 20°C

less than 500mm
500 – 750 mm
750 – 1500 mm
more than 1500 mm

storms, heavy rain, and large hailstones are typical of such systems in hot moist conditions.

It is important to ascertain not only the total rainfall for each month of the year, but also the maximum amount for any 24-hour period to be able to ensure adequate drainage from roofs (including gutters and downpipes) and paved areas. The designer must also determine whether there is any likelihood of driving rain and whether the building site is situated in a hail belt.

Climatic zones

By averaging a long series of accurate meteorological observations, the climates of different localities, or various features of them, can be compared with each other. Although there are of course innumerable 'local' climates, it has been found that

The hot climate zones of the world

Warm-wet

Wet and dry (composite)

Modified by altitude

Semi-arid

Arid desert

Sub-tropical Mediterranean

Sub-tropical humid

Highland variations

whole areas, far removed from each other, have striking similarities in their climatic patterns, and that the data for certain climatic elements in each area are very similar over a given period.

Rarely, if ever, do all the climatic elements have the same characteristics in different localities, no matter how similar their climates appear to be. By grouping climates into types, however, certain general truths about similar areas may stand out more clearly, and one can assess more easily the influences of those elements shared by these regions. Only those climates which are most likely to be unfamiliar to the European architect—the non-temperate or hot climates—will be discussed. For the purpose of this guide they have been divided into four main zones—warm-humid, wet and dry, hot-dry and sub-tropical—each with its major sub-divisions.

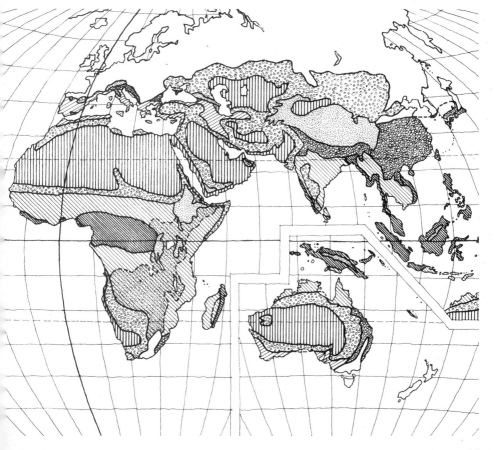

Characteristics of non-temperate climates

Warm-wet zones	Equatorial	Tropical marine (trade wind coasts)
Where found and vegetation	In lowlands within 5–10° of equator; may extend to higher latitudes on windward side of continents. Vegetation luxuriant and dense—quick growing and difficult to control.	Parts of tropical east coasts of Brazil, Central America, Madagascar, etc. Supports a rain forest vegetation very similar to lowlands near equator.
Seasonal variations	Little seasonal difference throughout the year—periods with more or less rain and the occasional dry spells, with clearer skies, are usually the hottest periods.	Little seasonal difference.
Air-temperature	Annual mean maximum day temperature in shade around 30°C. Annual mean minimum night temperature around 24°C. Both diurnal and annual ranges quite narrow: diurnal $\pm 8°C$, annual 1–3°C. The result is a monotonous similarity of temperature.	Maritime air exerts a moderating influence. Annual mean maximum day temperature in shade approximately 28°C. Annual mean minimum night temperature around 21°C. Diurnal range approximately as above, annual range small but rather greater than in equatorial regions.
Humidity	Humidity high during most of the year. Relative humidity about 75% for most of the time, but may vary from 55 to almost 100%. Vapour pressure remains steady in region of 2500–3000 N/m².	Fairly high constant humidity. Relative humidity varies between 55 and almost 100%. Vapour pressure between 1800–2500 N/m².
Precipitation	The mean annual rainfall is high and the daily incident of rain is very regular in each particular location—usually afternoon, often accompanied by violent electric storms. Total amount of rainfall can vary from 2000–5000 mm. May exceed	High annual rainfall—rainy periods often prolonged—1250–1750 mm. Up to 250 mm in wettest months.

(Left) Typical landscape of the warm-humid zone

(Right) Typical landscape of composite zone

	500 mm in wettest month and in heavy storm 50 mm or more can fall in an hour.	
Sky conditions and solar radiation	Fairly cloudy and hazy throughout year. Skies bright if cloud cover limited and sun not hidden. Solar radiation diffuse (reflected and scattered by cloud or high vapour content of air) but strong with sky glare. Reflected radiation from ground is low.	Clear skies and bright sun more frequent then equatorial zone. Dark and overcast before and during storms. Solar radiation strong and mainly direct with little diffusion when sky is clear.
Wind	Frequent periods of calm and winds, if any, are slight. Each place, however, is within the range of the trade winds for some period of the year.	On windward coasts persistent, moderately strong winds. The various cyclonic disturbances apt to be more severe than those of lower latitudes with occasional hurricanes.
General	High temperatures and humidity levels encourage insect breeding (mosquitoes and other insects abound), growth of fungi, rusting and rotting.	Hurricanes, with wind velocity of around 50 m/s or more constitute a serious seasonal hazard. Severe corrosion in coastal areas due to high salt content of air.
Note: Tropical wet monsoon	Parts of southern and eastern Asia, and a part of South America—tropical coasts backed by highlands. The rainfall of the wet season is so great that in spite of a short dry season these regions contain evergreen rainforests. This sub type is intermediate in character between Equatorial (see above) and Tropical continental (see below), for although it has high temperatures with a fairly small annual range, long periods with high humidity, and heavy rainfall, there is a marked dry season and marked season changes in wind direction.	

Warm-wet and hot-dry (composite) zones	Tropical continental or savanna	Tropical uplands
Where found and vegetation	Poleward of the warm-wet zones there is often a gradual transition to this type as the break between the rains increases in length. Vegetation	Extensive mountainous regions and plateaux (uplands over 1000 m above sea level) are to be found within the tropical continental zones. Vegeta-

	varies from the thorn scrub and tussocky grasses of the regions with lengthy droughts, through the park-like grasslands with numerous but scattered trees and bushes of the mid-savannas, to the closer woodlands and tall elephant grass where the dry period is of short duration.	tion luxurious to barren depending on latitude and altitude.
Seasonal variations	Normally two seasons: warm-wet during summer and hot-dry during winter. Often a third cool-dry season. In India, South-East Asia, and northern Australia the alternation of rainy and drought periods are part of monsoon systems and their climate is classified by some as Tropical monsoon, wet and dry, but it is fundamentally similar to that of the tropical continental zone.	Seasonal variations and climate generally similar to those of nearby lowlands but average temperatures fall below those of the lowlands. Heavy dew at night with ground frosts in winter. Hail storms and storms with violent electric discharges common.

Air temperature: In hottest parts of the year day temperatures may rise to over 40°C. Mean maximum temperatures in shade approximately 35°C (hot-dry season) and around 28°C (warm-wet season). Mean maximum night temperatures 24°C (dry season) and a degree or two higher during wet season. Night temperatures can fall to below 15°C during cool season. Fairly small mean annual range, mean diurnal range can be around 15°C (dry season) and 4°C (wet season).

Humidity: Fairly high humidity: during wet season RH 55–95 % and VP 2000–2500 N/m^2; during dry season RH 20–55 % and VP 1300–1600 N/m^2.

Precipitation: The rainfall amounts and the length of the dry season vary considerably. In wetter parts the rainfall is of the order of 1000–1500 mm, but on borders of the semi-arid lands less than 500 mm may fall in a year. Considerable local annual variations. Little or no rain during the dry season.

Sky conditions and solar radiation: Varied with season. Clear blue sky shortly after rainy season, but as dust content of air increases so does sky glare. Radiation—direct, diffused and from ground—moderate to high: alternates between conditions found in warm-wet and hot-dry zones.

Wind: Persistent, strong wind (which can be dusty) abating towards the end of the dry season.

General: Great seasonal changes in humidity cause swelling and shrinkage of moisture-absorbing materials which can result in rapid weakening. Termites are common. Dust and sand storms may occur.

Hot-dry zones	**Arid desert**	**Semi-arid**
Where found and vegetation	These climates prevail on the western sides of land masses between 20–25°N and S (extremes 15–30°N and S). Vegetation extremely sparse—cactus and sage-bush can survive, other plants lie dormant in the seed waiting for rare rainfall.	Low latitude steppes (a) occur on the equatorial sides of the deserts. Vegetation sparse. Poleward of hot-deserts are semi-arid areas (b) with coarse grasses and certain plants.
Seasonal variations	Two seasons: a hot and somewhat cooler period.	(a) Resembles arid type with a long dry season and a short rainy season

22

South Yemen—typical
desert landscape

during summer. As rain is in hottest months (yearly amount variable but usually under 500 mm) when evaporation is at maximum it is not very effective for plant growth.

(b) Resembles arid type but dry and very hot summer months and variable annual rainfall in winter months which is more effective for plant growth.

Air temperature

Mean maximum day temperature in shade around 45°C during summer (in places shade temperatures of over 50°C may be reached) and between 20–30° in winter. Night-time mean around 25°C during summer, and between 10–20°C in the cool season. Diurnal range of 20°C not uncommon. Annual range depends on latitude—with increasing latitude winters relatively colder and annual range greater.

Humidity

Humidity low. RH fluctuates with air temperature—can range from below 20 % in afternoon to over 40 % at night. VP fairly steady, varying with location and season from about 500–1500 N/m². Maritime areas experience high humidity— RH steadily high between 50 and 90 % with VP of 1500–2000 N/m²; which offshore/onshore breeze only partly counteracts.

Precipitation

Rains are few and far between—precipitation sometimes starts at high altitudes, but evaporates before it reaches the ground. Large areas average between 50–150 mm per year. Averages mean little as years may pass with absolute drought, while a sudden storm may bring 50 mm in an hour.

Sky conditions and solar radiation

The sky is without cloud for the greater part of the year, but dust haze and storms are frequent, occurring mainly in the afternoon.
Direct solar radiation is intense and is augmented by radiation reflected from the barren, light-coloured terrain.

Wind

Winds usually local: generally low in morning increasing towards noon to reach a maximum in the afternoon, frequently accompanied by whirlwinds of sand and dust.

General

Materials and structures can crack as a result of the high diurnal temperature difference. Dust and sand-storms can, in addition to being a considerable nuisance, have a harmful effect on building materials.

23

Sub-tropical zones— thermal transition zones between the temperate zones and the tropics:	**Mediterranean**	**Humid**
	Where found and vegetation	
	On the western side of continents centred about latitudes 35N and S. Variability quite large. Can be divided into 3 subtypes: marine, continental and mountainous. Vegetation: forest trees, mainly scattered, widespread. In areas of limestone, low scrub and heath. In Europe distribution of olive tree corresponds to extent of zone.	This climate is found mainly in the eastern parts of continents between latitudes 25–40 N and S. Vegetation generally luxuriant, though not as dense as the warm-wet zones, with many smaller trees and shrubs occupying the lower levels. In areas with more moderate rainfall grasses may replace trees eg over much of the Argentine Pampas and Uruguay.
Seasonal variations	Broad climatic pattern one of very warm to hot summers with abundant sunshine and little rain, and mild winters with moderate rainfall.	Rain in all seasons although there is usually a summer maximum—many parts of the south-eastern USA west of the Mississippi have a slight winter maximum. Summers are distinctly warm to hot and humid with nights as uncomfortable as the days, while winters are relatively mild and pleasant.
Air temperatures	Mid-summer temperatures vary with location but mean monthly values of 20–25°C are usual (30°C and over in continental areas, lower in marine locations). Diurnal range in continental areas large (15–18°C); small in marine locations (5–10°C). Midwinter average tends to be between 7–13°C, night temperature may fall to near, and occasionally below, freezing.	There are fairly wide differences in temperatures between one part of the climatic region and another depending on local relief, latitude, nearness to the sea and other factors. Mean maximum summer day temperature in the shade in the order of 25–30°C; during winter the maximum day temperatures usually average between 6–20°C. The humid atmosphere and, often, cloudy skies result in

24

(Left) Sub-tropical
Mediterranean—the
Greek island of Skyros

(Right) Sub-tropical
humid—the Natal coast
of South Africa

		relatively small diurnal ranges of about 7–10°C.
Humidity	RH very variable ranging from 40–90%. VP in summer high in marine locations—about 2000–2200 N/m²—and moderately low in continental areas—1500 N/m².	RH high in summer with mean values between 70–80%. Not only are the days hot and sultry but the nights are oppressive as well. RH in winter between 40–70%.
Precipitation	Rainfall amounts also vary a great deal from wetter marine sites (about 500 mm per annum) to sheltered inland locations with a smaller average (about 300 mm but very variable).	Rainfall is plentiful, though the annual total varies between 800–1800 mm according to location. Summer convection causes many tropical downpours and thunderstorms are common.
Sky conditions and solar radiation	Clear skies with periodical light cloud cover. Fairly high direct solar radiation, moderate diffused radiation from clouds and moderate to high radiation reflected from ground.	Fairly cloudy throughout year. Solar radiation largely diffuse but relatively strong with sky glare.
Wind	Mainly from westerly direction; tends to be relatively strong starting in late morning, reaching maximum in the afternoon. Nights almost calm.	Winds too vary according to location. Generally speaking, in summer, winds off the nearby oceans bring much rain in the form of heavy thunder-showers. In winter, the return monsoon-type winds off the cool continents are dry. During the spring and autumn seasons, typhoons and hurricanes come up the coasts from the edges of the tropical zones; they cause strong winds and heavy rains. Several local winds are important eg the violent 'pampero' which strikes the Pampas of Argentina in summer, the 'southerly Bursters' in Australia and the hot north-west wind in Natal.

General

Dust can sometimes accompany winds in the inland areas. Corrosion in marine locations.

High temperature and humidity levels encourage growth of fungi, rusting, rotting and insects. Hurricanes constitute a serious seasonal hazard in America and Asia. There are a large number of electric storms in many parts of the zone.

Comfort

As one of the primary functions of any building is to counteract at least some of the main disadvantages of the climate in which it is situated, it should be able to filter, absorb or repel climatic and other elements according to their adverse or beneficial contributions to the comfort of its inhabitants or users.

Although human comfort cannot be measured in terms of psychological factors only, one of the primary requirements (and this is particularly true in the hot climatic zones) is the maintenance of thermal balance between the human body and its environment. This involves keeping the internal temperature of the body within a certain range, regardless of the relatively wide variations in the external environment. The conditions under which such balance is achieved, and the state of the body when it reaches equilibrium with the surroundings, depend on the combined effect of many factors; some, such as the activity, acclimatisation and clothing of the subject are individual characteristics, while others, such as the air temperature, radiation, humidity and air movement are environmental factors.

Thermal exchange between human body and its environment

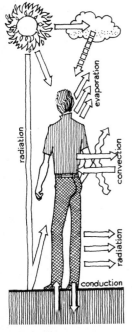

The body maintains a constant internal temperature by releasing superfluous heat to the environment and there is, as a result, a continuous exchange of heat between the body and its surroundings which may take place in four physically different ways—conduction, convection, radiation and evaporation. These physical processes depend on the climate and are influenced in particular by the four afore-mentioned environmental factors, each of which may aid of impede the dissipation of surplus heat from the body.

The contribution that conduction makes to the heat exchange process depends first and foremost on the thermal conductivity of the materials in immediate contact with the skin. A clothed person does not normally lose any great amount of heat by conduction and the physiological significance of heat loss by this process is limited to the local cooling of particular parts of the body when they come in contact with the cold materials that

26

are good conductors. This is of practical importance in the choice of flooring and surface materials of all kinds.

The body exchanges heat with the surrounding air by convection. This form of heat exchange depends primarily on the temperature difference between the skin and air, and how much the air is moving. Long-wave radiation, on the other hand, takes place between the human body and surrounding surfaces such as walls and windows. In this process the temperature, humidity, and movement of the air have practically no influence on the amount of heat transmitted, which depends in the main on the difference in temperature between the skin and the surfaces that surround or enclose it.

The body may gain or lose heat by these processes depending on whether the environment is colder or warmer than the body surface—in cold conditions the skin temperature is higher than the air temperature, while in hot countries the situation is reversed.

When the surrounding temperature (air and walls) is above 25°C, the clothed human body cannot get rid of enough heat by either convection or radiation and the loss of perspiration becomes the sole compensatory mechanism. Water consumes heat in order to evaporate, and as humans normally lose about one litre of water a day in perspiration, a fair amount of heat is taken from the body to evaporate it. The extent to which heat is lost by evaporation depends on the clothing worn, the levels of surrounding vapour pressure and the amount of air movement. The lower the vapour pressure and the more the air movement, the greater will be the evaporative potential. This is, however, lessened by clothing which reduces the air movement and increases the humidity over the skin.

Comfort zone

The range of conditions in which thermal comfort is experienced is called the comfort zone—something which differs with individuals and is affected by the clothing worn, geographical location, age and sex. Although the comfort zone is defined as a subjective assessment of the environmental conditions, the limits of the zone do have a physiological basis; the range of conditions under which the thermo-regulatory mechanisms of the body are in a state of minimal activity. Comfort, which is also dependent on not only the air temperature and that of the surrounding surfaces, but also on the relative humidity of the air and air movement, cannot be expressed in terms of any one

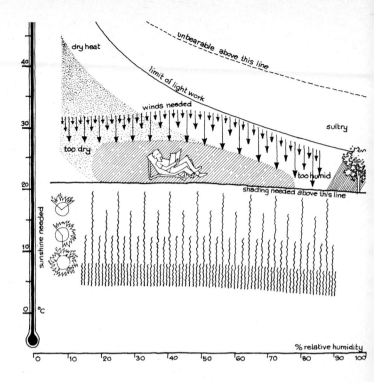

of them as they affect the body simultaneously and the influence of any one depends on the levels of the other factors. Several attempts have been made to evaluate the combined effects of these factors on the physiological and sensory response of the body and to express any combination of them in terms of a single parameter or 'thermal index' which can be set out on a nomogram.

Climate and comfort: design aids

Victor Olgyay (*Design with Climate*) was the first to propose a systematic procedure for adapting the design of a building to human requirements and climatic conditions. His method is based on a Bioclimatic Chart on which comfort zones—one for summer and one for winter—can be determined for the climatic region to which it is to be applied. Once this has been done any climatic condition, determined by its dry-bulb temperature and humidity, can then be plotted on the chart: comfort requirements can be evaluated; deviations from the comfort zone, and whether these can be eliminated by natural means, can be ascertained.

The relation of indoor to outdoor conditions, however, varied widely with different characteristics of building construction

28

and design, and as Givoni points out in his book *Man, Climate and Architecture*, the Bioclimatic Chart is therefore limited in its applicability as the analysis of physiological requirements is based on the outdoor climate and not on that expected within the building in question. He has proposed an alternative method which uses one of the thermal indices to evaluate the human requirements for comfort, from which the necessary features of building design to achieve this comfort are determined. This method involves an estimation of the indoor climate expected and for practical use the suitability of ventilation, air temperature reduction, and evaporative cooling—for ambient conditions combining different temperature ranges and vapour pressures—are plotted on an involved diagram to form what has been named a Building Bioclimatic Chart.

Well designed buildings can provide comfortable conditions without the use of expensive, energy-consuming mechanical equipment. This is only possible, however, if climate is taken into account from the outset; if it is taken into account when deciding on the over-all concept, on the layout and orientation, and on the shape and character of structures among other things. Unfortunately, most of the methods which the designer can use to help to solve the climatic problems are cumbersome and time consuming and to overcome this difficulty the Mahoney Tables were developed by the Department of Development and Tropical Studies of the Architectural Association. With this method a number of the most easily accessible climatic data are assembled and entered in simple tables which help the designer to formulate recommendations for those features that must be decided during the sketch plan stage.

.ocal environment

The effects of the local environment on the way of living and traditional way of building must be considered; the more severe the climate the more important does this become. Although it would be wrong to romanticise the accomplishments of the native builders—there are many examples of almost anti-climatic solutions—and a mistake to imitate their construction techniques and forms, a great deal can be learned from a study of the principles they applied. Traditional solutions will be discussed under the various headings in the section which follows.

Some measure of relief from climatic stress can be obtained

Humid Indicators

H1 indicates that air movement is essential. It applies when high temperature (day thermal stress = H) is combined with high humidity (HG = 4) or when the high temperature (day thermal stress = H) is combined with moderate humidity (HG = 2 or 3) and a small diurnal range (DR less than 10°C);

H2 indicates that air movement is desirable. It applies when temperatures within the comfort limits are combined with high humidity (HG = 4);

H3 indicates that precautions against rain penetration are needed. Problems may arise even with low precipitation figures, but will be inevitable when rainfall exceeds 200 mm per month.

Arid Indicators

A1 indicates the need for thermal storage. It applies when a large diurnal range (10°C or more) coincides with moderate or low humidity (HG = 1, 2 or 3);

A2 indicates the desirability of outdoor sleeping space. It is needed when the night temperature is high (night thermal stress = H) and the humidity is low (HG = 1 or 2). It may be needed also when nights are comfortable outdoors but hot indoors as a result of heavy thermal storage (ie, day = H, humidity group = 1 or 2 and when the diurnal range is above 10°C);

A3 indicates winter or cool-season problems. These occur when the day temperature falls below the comfort limits (day thermal stress = C);

The Mahoney Tables provide a guide to design in relation to climate using readily available climatic data. A step by step procedure leads one from the climatic information to specifications for optimal conditions of layout etc needed at sketch design stage. The analysis requires the use of four tables which determine certain indicator totals for humidity (H) and aridity (A)—these are transferred to Table 5 and the appropriate recommendation for each of 8 subjects is found

SKETCH DESIGN RECOMMENDATIONS

Indicator totals from table 4						Recommendations
Humid			Arid			
H1	H2	H3	A1	A2	A3	
						Layout
			0–10			1. Buildings orientated on east-west axis to reduce exposure to sun
			11 or 12	5–12		
					0–4	2. Compact courtyard planning
						Spacing
11 or 12						3. Open spacing for breeze penetration
2–10						4. As 3, but protect from cold/hot wind
0 or 1						5. Compact planning
						Air movement
3–12						6. Rooms single banked. Permanent provision for air movement
1 or 2			0–5			
			6–12			7. Double-banked rooms with temporary provision for air movement
0		2–12				
		0 or 1				8. No air movement requirement
						Openings
		0 to 1			0	9. Large openings, 40–80% of N and S walls
		11 or 12			0 or 1	10. Very small openings, 10–20%
		Any other conditions				11. Medium openings, 20–40%
						Walls
			0–2			12. Light walls; short time lag
			3–12			13. Heavy external and internal walls
						Roofs
			0–5			14. Light insulated roofs
			6–12			15. Heavy roofs; over 8 hours' time lag
						Outdoor sleeping
				2–12		16. Space for outdoor sleeping required
						Rain protection
		3–12				17. Protection from heavy rain needed

through skilful design, but comfortable living is often assisted by adaptation of individual life-style which the designer must also take into consideration. It would be impossible to describe here the effect of climate on life-styles in all the zones under review. One example, however, should suffice to illustrate this point. Allan Rodgers, in his article, The Sudanese Heat Trap, explains how the living patterns in the hot, arid Sudan change through the year in response to the changes in climate.

In summer, work begins early while the day is cool and continues till shortly after midday when a break is taken so that people can rest during the hottest part of the afternoon. At this time of the day the internal temperature of their houses is still well below the outside air temperature and the buildings can be well used during the rest period. When activity restarts later in the afternoon the outside temperature is past its peak but the indoor temperature is still rising, so people tend to move outdoors, spending time in courtyards, patios, and gardens where they also usually sleep at this time of the year. As soon as it becomes cooler outside than in, the small shuttered windows and the external doors are opened to enable air to blow through and assist in cooling the interior. Ventilation is continued until shortly after sunrise when all the openings are once again sealed up in order to exclude the hot, dust-laden outdoor air. In winter, on the other hand, when night can become extremely cold, it is usual to sleep indoors with only very limited ventilation.

Chapter 2

Design and climate

Site climate

It is obvious that a building in the tropics should differ from one situated in the temperate zone, but it is less obvious that even in the same area—city, town, village or rural area—there are microclimatic differences which should be recognised in the design and construction of buildings. As a result of various influences the air temperature in an urban area, for example, can be as much as 8°C higher than in the surrounding countryside, while the relative humidity can be 5–10 per cent lower.

Climatic design is based on typical or normal weather conditions and it is usually relatively easy for the designer to obtain the necessary meteorological data for any given region from a variety of published material. Unlike regional climate data, however, site climate information is not readily available and will have to be acquired through personal observation and local experience. Some of the more important factors which may cause local variations and which the designer must consider are:

Topography

The shape, orientation, exposure, elevation, and hills or valleys at or near the site must be investigated as they can have an effect on not only temperature but also the distribution of solar radiation, wind and precipitation. The influence of small hills (changes in ground level of 300 m or more) on rainfall patterns can be quite pronounced, for instance, particularly when moisture bearing winds blow regularly from the same direction. The windward slope in this case can be expected to receive a rainfall of more than the regional average and the leeward slope correspondingly less. The higher or steeper the hill, the greater will be the effect.

Temperature in the atmosphere decreases with altitude (7–8 m in height can cause a difference of 5°C in air temperature in still conditions) and this can be important in hot lands where temperatures may be more favourable at higher elevations.

The grass huts of the humid tropics where an open construction is vital to ensure continuous ventilation

At night, however, this effect is reversed as cold air drains down to the lowest points. In hot climate zones this fact can be used to advantage by the designer as a raised embankment, wall or

33

fairly impermeable hedge on the lower side of a site can dam up the cool air which flows slowly down the slope. It would, of course, be desirable to provide a gate or use a deciduous hedge so that the flow of air is not blocked during the winter. If, on the other hand, it is necessary to protect a site from undesirable wind caused by flow of air down-slope, a wall or hedge running diagonally across the slope above the site would deflect the air stream. In this case a barrier running horizontally across the slope would not afford adequate protection since the air dammed up in this way would eventually overflow in a rush.

Water   The proximity of bodies of water can moderate extreme temperature variations; land on the lee side of water will be warmer in winter and cooler in summer. Humidity may also be affected, depending on the general temperature pattern. The larger the body of water, the greater its impact on the microclimate.

In summer, during the daytime, the earth heats up considerably in comparison with the water; the hot air rises and cool air must flow in to replace it. The shores of lakes and oceans as a result benefit from a daytime breeze, blowing from the water to the land, which has a cooling effect felt for between 400–800 m inland. At night the air over land cools faster than that over the water and the process is reversed, with the breeze blowing from the land to the water. Experiments done on a clear winter night have shown that temperatures gradually decrease as one moves away from a lake shore.

Ground surface   The portion of solar radiation which reaches the earth raises the temperature of the ground—the amount depends on latitude, the season, the slope of the ground, the hour of the day and the nature of the terrain—and during the daytime the highest temperature is always found at the boundary between the ground and the air. The temperature, in other words, increases considerably as one approaches the ground. At night, as a result of the loss of heat by evaporation and the effective outgoing radiation, the reverse is true and the temperature decreases as one approaches the ground. A peculiarity of microclimate, therefore, is that the closer one approaches the ground the more extreme it becomes.

The natural cover of a terrain tends to moderate extreme temperatures and stabilise conditions. Plant and grassy cover

34

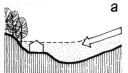

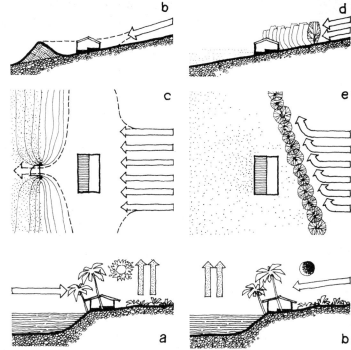

(Above and right) At night cold air drains to lowest point (**a**) and can be dammed up by an embankment (**b**) which should have an opening for use in cold periods (**c**). A diagonal barrier can be used to protect buildings from undesirable breezes (**d** and **e**)

(Right) The direction of breezes between water and land at seashore and lakeside locations (see text)

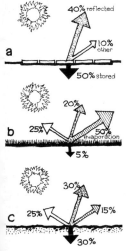

(Above) Absorption of heat by different surface materials—paving (**a**), grass (**b**) and bare ground (**c**)

(Right) The temperatures in and around buildings can be tempered or aggravated by the nature of surrounding surfaces. Temperatures shown were recorded in hot-dry climate when the air temperature was 42°C

reduces temperatures and while they may be still further reduced by other vegetation, cities and man-made surfaces tend to elevate temperatures and reduce humidity. A fairly common mistake, which can have most unpleasant results in hot climate zones, is to place paved surfaces—which store up a great deal more heat and remain hot longer than unpaved or grass surfaces—close to the windows of houses and other buildings. Not only do these paved areas add appreciable heat to the air layer near their surface, but they also radiate and reflect large amounts of heat into the building, possibly aggravating already uncomfortable conditions.

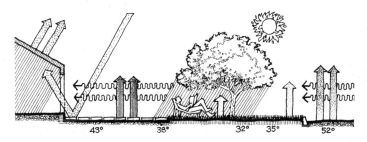

Vegetation

In all hot-dry zones the beneficial effect of even the lightest plant cover is quite considerable and all existing plants should be taken into account by the designer. Vegetation also provides protection against glare, dust and erosion. It can, on the other hand, have disadvantages when it is too close to a building, as roots can damage foundations and drain pipes, leaves can block gutters, and desirable air movement can be drastically reduced or directed away over the building.

(Top right) A vortex is formed in front of a building standing square to the wind resulting in unpleasant winds at ground level (**a**) which can be reduced by a canopy (**b**). A low building immediately windward increases the problem (**c**). Velocity at ground level between low buildings is usually less than wind velocity (**d**)

(Bottom right) Wind movement in defined openings and in thinned forest areas.

In forests both winter and summer average daily temperatures drop by a few degrees. In the daytime, when the top of the forest is being strongly heated by solar radiation, what cool air there is—being heavier than the warmer air—sinks down to the ground level. The leaves of the trees re-radiate heat at night in a manner similar to that of bare ground and this produces cooling with the cooled air once again sinking to ground level. As a result of these processes there is a very uniform temperature at the ground surface of a forest. These conditions, however, occur only *within* a forest and normal variations are produced in large clearings and at the borders. Small clearings, on the other hand, can create problems and it has been found that they tend to possess microclimates of greater extremes than nearby open country.

Windbreaks

(Below) Wind velocity gradients; urban areas (**a**), wooded countryside (**b**) and open country (**c**). In **d** and **e** one can see there is an area (A) of reduced velocity on the windward side of a windbreak. Behind it the greatest shelter begins at a distance of 4 or 5 times the height of the break.

Physical features such as neighbouring buildings, walls, trees etc, which may influence air movement or cast shadows, must be taken into account. There is a difference between the shelter offered by windbreaks composed of plants and that offered by solid screens or buildings, as the extent of shelter depends not only on height but also on the degree of permeability. Plant material, which permits a certain amount of air to pass through, causes less turbulence than solid screens and, as a result, a greater total area of shelter.

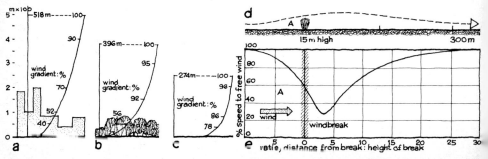

36

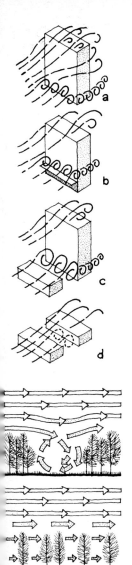

The zone just behind the windbreak itself is that with the greatest protection from the wind, and the lowest wind speed is found at a distance of about three or four times the height of the screen depending on its openness. The more impenetrable the screen, the shorter is the distance to the point of minimum wind speed and the greater is the reduction in velocity. Although windbreaks are normally used to protect buildings from cold winter winds, care must be taken that cooling summer breezes are not blocked.

Air movement or winds are equally affected by buildings whose length, height and roof pitch all influence the wind patterns and in so doing have a distinct impact on the surrounding microclimate. The same is true of groups of buildings, and great care should be taken with their layout to minimise any channelling (or funnelling) effects which can more than double the velocity and cause strong turbulences and eddies to be set up.

In forests the wind speed can be 25–50 per cent of the speed found outside and defined openings cut into the forest or a general thinning of the area without any well-defined openings can result in quite different wind flow conditions. In the case of defined openings, eddies can result and the prevailing wind near the surface may flow in the opposite direction to that above the trees. In thinned forest areas, however, winds are usually in the same direction all the way down to the ground, although the speed is still greatly reduced.

Site climatic conditions must be studied in order to identify the area most suitable for buildings (particularly on a large site) and to take advantage of the favourable existing microclimatic variations if they are recognised. It must, on the other hand, be remembered that although the general climate is essentially unalterable, the climate of a specific portion of the land can be influenced easily and altered by design. The immediate environment of a building (or group of buildings) can, in other words, be wilfully manipulated through earth mounds, walls, planting, pools, siting and building forms among other things.

Orientation

The orientation of a building is determined by the climatic factors of wind (discussed in more detail further on) and solar radiation as well as by the view, noise and requirements of privacy which may, at times, override the climatic con-

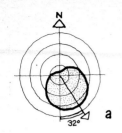

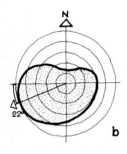

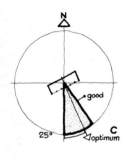

(Above) The total radiation during the underheated period (**a**) and during the overheated period (**b**) for Arizona. From the diagrams it can be seen that a compromise must be made to determine the optimum orientation (**c**)

Form

(Below) East and west facing walls should normally be kept as short as possible

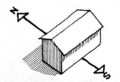

siderations. The orientation of a building is affected by the quantities of solar radiation falling on different sides at different times. It has, however, been recognised that both radiation and temperature act together to produce the heat experienced by a body or surface. This is expressed as the sol-air temperature, which includes three component temperatures: firstly that of the outdoor air; secondly, the solar radiation absorbed by the body or surface and, lastly, the long-wave radiant heat exchange with the environment.

In his book *Design with Climate*, Olgyay describes a sol-air approach to orientation in which not only the radiation receipts are considered, but also the heat impact of the diurnal temperatures. In hot climate areas protection from solar radiation is particularly important during times of excessive heat when there can be a difference of as much as 3°C in air temperature in a building between the worst and best orientation. Optimum orientation would reduce radiation to a minimum in the so-called overheated period, while simultaneously allowing some radiation during the cool months or the underheated period.

By plotting the directions of maximum radiant gain for both hot and cool months, it is possible to determine the optimum orientation for any given location. It is unlikely that the two directions will be at right angles to each other and some compromise must be made in order to achieve the most satisfactory distribution of total heat receipts in all seasons. It is difficult to generalise, but as east and west facing walls receive the highest intensities of radiation they should normally be kept as short as possible and openings, if they must be used on these sides, should be as small as possible. The west side, which receives its maximum radiation during the hottest part of the day, can be particularly troublesome.

It can be taken as a rule that the optimum shape is that which has the minimum heat gain in summer and the minimum heat loss in winter. From his radiation calculations in different environmental situations, Olgyay feels that a square building is not the optimal shape anywhere, although it is more efficient in both summer and winter than shapes elongated in a north-south direction. He concludes that in every case the most satisfactory shape is one in which the building is elongated in some general east-west direction.

38

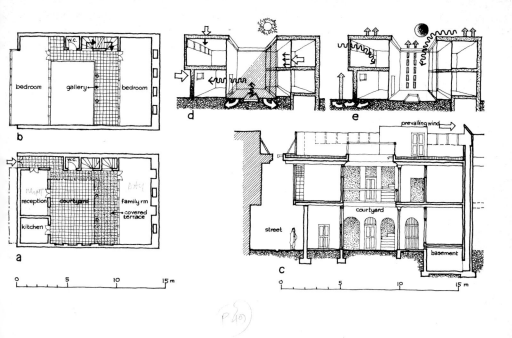

b

a

c

d

e

prevailing wind

bedroom | gallery | bedroom

reception | courtyard | family rm

kitchen | covered terrace

street | courtyard | basement

Typical oriental courtyard house in Iraq. Ground floor plan (**a**), first floor plan (**b**) and section (**c**). The diagrammatic sections (**d** and **e**) illustrate the thermal system of this type of building, showing how the shaded courtyard provides a source of cool air during the daytime

Once again it is difficult to generalise. For example, although the winter conditions in hot, arid regions would permit an elongated house design, the heat stress in summer is so severe that a compromise is required and the traditional solution is a compact, inward looking building with an interior courtyard. This minimises the solar radiation impact on the outside walls and provides a cool area within the building. In Iraq, for instance, the courtyard has remained a dominant element for centuries and excavations at Ur show that similar layouts were used as far back as 2000BC. Subhi Hussein Al-Azzawi, in an article, Oriental Houses in Iraq, shows that the courtyard is spatially the focal point and acts as an extension to surrounding covered terraces and the rooms beyond. The covered terraces which are usually on two or three sides of the courtyard, and the identical covered gallery on the first floor, help to reduce the quantity of heat gained during the day and provide shaded areas. As the height of the court is usually greater than any of its dimensions on plan there is always adequate shading, even when the summer sun is almost directly overhead. When the courtyard is provided with water and plants it acts as a cooling well and modifies the microclimate. The use of these elements also helps to raise the very low humidity of the air to a more comfortable level, and is often supplemented by spraying water on to the courtyard floor several times a day.

The warm-humid environment, on the other hand, emphasises the need for shade, for elimination of radiation conditions on the east and west walls, and the need to catch whatever air movement there is. This suggests marked east-west elongation of the building, but if protective shade is available, considerable freedom is possible in building shapes and orientation to ensure that advantage is taken of any prevailing winds.

Structure

There is a continuous exchange of heat between a building and its outdoor environment. The factors affecting this transmission are convection (which depends on the rate of ventilation), radiation through windows, evaporation—all of which will be discussed under the following headings—and conduction which may occur through the walls and roof inwards or outwards; this includes the effect of solar radiation on these surfaces.

The amount of heat penetrating a building depends largely on the nature of the walls and roof. In the hot period of the day heat flows through these elements into the building where some of it is stored; at night, during the cool period, the flow is reversed. When appropriate properties are chosen it is possible to achieve and maintain comfortable internal temperatures over a wide range of external conditions. The materials and type of construction to be used must be assessed in terms of the following:

Absorptivity/ emissivity

Especially important in hot climate areas. Radiation striking an opaque surface may be absorbed or reflected. The colour of a surface gives a good indication of its absorptivity for solar radiation which decreases, and the reflectivity increases, with lightness. In other words the darker the colour of a surface, the higher its temperature will be raised by the absorption of solar energy. Colour, however, does not indicate the behaviour of a surface with regard to its emissivity or power to emit long-wave radiation and both black and white painted surfaces lose heat to the sky at night at equal rates.

Materials which reflect rather than absorb radiation and which more readily release the absorbed quantity as thermal radiation will cause lower temperatures with the structure.

Porousness

With increased moisture content, materials show higher heat

transmittance because of the relatively high thermal conductivity of water.

Insulation value

As air is one of the best insulators, materials which enclose or contain air have low heat transfer characteristics and generally are light in weight. Insulation is most effective under steady state conditions or if the direction of heat flow is constant for long periods.

Walls, roofs and building components are often made up of two or more layers separated by air spaces which provide a resistance to heat flow. The amount of this resistance depends not only on the width of the air space but also on the characteristics of the enclosing surfaces as heat transfer across these spaces takes place mainly by radiation from one surface to another. For this reason highly reflective materials, such as metal foil, used in air spaces can reduce their thermal conductance by over two- or even threefold in some instances. Heat exchange by conduction and convection in the air space depends on whether the space is horizontal or vertical, on its width and on the direction of the heat flow (upwards, downwards or horizontal).

Thermal capacity

Or the heat storage value. The larger this is, the slower the temperature change that is propagated through the material. This delay is called the 'time lag' of the construction and materials with large time lags are usually dense in quality and heavy in weight. Under conditions with large diurnal temperature variations the significance of thermal capacity is much greater than that of insulation.

Solar radiation affects buildings in two ways, however; it is not only absorbed by the wall and roof surfaces, but also enters through glazed areas which transmit solar or short-wave radiation with very little loss in heat energy. As a result of the greenhouse effect—glass allows the short-wave solar radiation to pass through but not the long-wave radiation emitted by objects or surfaces in a room—the heat which enters through glazed areas is trapped and can increase the indoor temperature to far above that of the air outdoors. The indiscriminate use of glass in hot climate areas can, therefore, not be recommended although by taking certain precautions (discussed further on), the various advantages, aesthetic and otherwise, of using transparent material can be utilised.

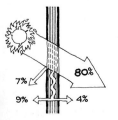

Solar heat gain through a single sheet of clear glass

7%
9%
80%
4%

41

A wide range of special heat-absorbing and heat-reflecting glasses are available on the market, but most of them are limited in their effectiveness because either their own temperature is raised, which increases the heat convected and re-radiated into the internal space, or they tend to reduce even more light than heat.

The principles of thermal control through structure and material use are well illustrated by the way native builders exploit the limited materials available to them and work them into structural forms that admirably meet the demands of climate.

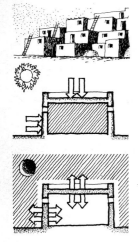

To modify the extremes of the diurnal range and to insulate the interior from the blistering heat outside, buildings in hot-dry zones are traditionally constructed with thick walls and roofs, and with very small openings. The thick exterior walls and roof—most often built of materials with a high heat capacity such as clay and stone, which are plentiful in these regions—absorb solar radiation during the daylight hours and slowly re-radiate it during the night. In this way the external temperatures are damped, and internal temperatures stabilised, being cooler in daytime and warmer at night. The mass of the wall structure is adjusted to meet climatic extremes. In regions where diurnal and seasonal variations are not so large and the intense direct and reflected radiation is the main source of discomfort, the wall mass is often reduced with the outside surfaces painted white, or some other light colour, to reflect a maximum of the radiant heat. By contrast, in some areas of extreme diurnal temperature variation truly monolithic houses are built to increase heat capacity, and in places are even built into cliff

(Above) Monolithic dwellings with small openings in hot-dry climates. Heat is stored in walls during the daytime when the inside is cooler than the outside; during the cool evenings the heat radiated inward warms the interior

A vaulted roof in the hot-dry zone—a curved roof has a larger convection heat-transfer area and is cooled more easily than a flat one

faces or underground.

Although flat roofs are practical in areas where it seldom rains, the great tradition for roofing in desert regions is the vault or dome. As Victor Olgyay has explained, this has an underlying logic which was probably discovered through centuries of experience: as the rounded form of a hemispherical vault has a larger surface area than its base, solar radiation is diluted and re-radiation during the evenings is also greatly facilitated.

In the warm-wet regions heavy rainfall and high humidity are combined with relatively moderate air temperature and high solar radiation, so that shade and maximum ventilation are the critical components of comfort. Traditional shelters are most often very open in plan and construction, and one problem of the openness—necessary both day and night—is that with the small diurnal temperature range, little reduction in internal temperature is possible. The heat capacity of the structure must, therefore, be as low as possible to prevent accumulation of heat during the daytime, and to minimise re-radiation, which can cause discomfort at night when air movement is at its lowest.

To lessen the heat-retaining capacity of the structure and maximise the air flow across the interior, the native people in most areas of this zone reduce the wall to a minimum or eliminate it altogether. The roof becomes the dominant element in these houses and acts as a large umbrella; usually of thick thatch and steeply sloped, it both insulates the living space below from the heat of the sun, and allows the torrential rains to be shed quickly and almost silently. It also avoids condensation problems by being able to 'breathe'.

Above) Typical airy, open shelter found in the humid zone where good ventilation and protection from rain are essential

In the traditional Japanese house ventilation can be obtained during the oppressively hot and humid summer months by opening the large sliding *shoji* screens

Shade

(Below right) A shading device can not only reflect heat on to a building but also trap hot air as well as cause heat to be conducted inwards through the structure (**a**). These problems can be avoided through careful design and detailing (**b**)

The impact of solar radiation on buildings in hot climates must be reduced not only by orientation and effective design of the structure, but also by adequate shading. Although it is not always convenient or economical to shade roofs, walls lend themselves to this treatment in a number of ways which can be invaluable for eliminating or reducing one of the greatest sources of heat gain; the solar radiation entering through windows. Various methods are available for screening walls and windows, and when deciding on the shading requirements each facade must be separately considered to achieve the most effective solar control.

Vegetation

Existing trees and shrubs provide the simplest way of protecting a low building (or part of it) from solar radiation. Deciduous trees are especially valuable as they do not cut out winter sunshine.

Horizontal screens

(Below) Horizontal, vertical and egg-crate type shading devices

(Below centre) Overhangs should exclude sun during summer and, if necessary, admit it in winter (**a**). If a building is situated between the tropics shading of both the north and south walls must be considered (**b**)

Are most effective against a high sun and are normally used on the north or south sides. The nearer one is to the equator, the easier it is to screen these facades with a roof overhang such as those most often used in the warm-wet regions. The overhangs are generally sufficient to protect the interior of the dwelling from slanting sun and driving rain, as well as to provide shade over some portion of the surrounding area throughout the day. Balconies and projecting floor slabs are also common forms of horizontal screening.

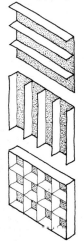

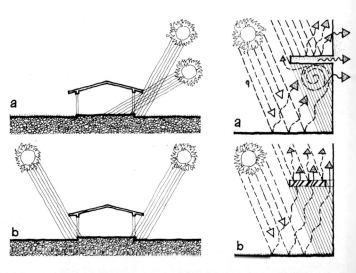

(Right) Flap on external shutters provides shading for that part of the window not protected by the roof overhang

(Below left) A solid horizontal canopy with some of the problems of shading devices illustrated on the previous page. (Note flyscreen on exterior of louvred windows. This type of screen can reduce the ventilation rate considerably. See Chapter 3.)

Open egg-crate type horizontal canopy

Vertical screens

In the form of closely spaced columns, vertical fins or rotating louvres are useful against the low sun on the east and west facades.

Combined vertical and horizontal screening—the egg-crate grill, for example—can be effective for any orientation depending on its depths and the dimensions of the openings. Whatever type of screening is used it should be placed outside the glazing, be of low thermal capacity materials to ensure quick cooling after sunset, and should be designed to prevent not only reflection on to any part of the building but also hot air becoming trapped.

45

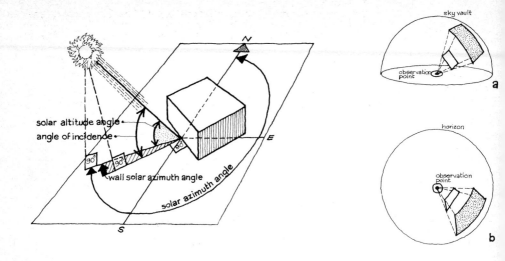

solar altitude angle
angle of incidence
wall solar azimuth angle
solar azimuth angle

N
E
S

sky vault
observation point
a

horizon
observation point
b

Solar charts devised for several countries and a shadow angle protractor can be used to calculate shadow requirements and check the efficiency of the proposed screening for any orientation, for any time of the day, any day of the year. The method of using these charts is described in detail in various books and will not be repeated here. A shading mask can also be produced using a shadow angle protractor. Any solid object placed between the sun and the centre of the diagram (point of observation) will cast a shadow on this point. The situation can also be reversed with the same effect; the light source can be placed at the point of observation and the shadow is then cast on to the sky vault. The areas of the sky vault covered by the shadow are then the portions of the sky from which no light can reach the point of observation as long as the solid or opaque object is present. If the sun itself moves through such an area of the sky vault, clearly the point of observation will then be in shade and receive no direct light from the sun.

Any object of regular geometrical lines has a characteristic shading mask, which represents the section of the sky which it will obscure. In many cases, different shading devices will leave similar masks so that several possible solutions to a shading problem will exist. The designer, in other words, may decide early in the process what shading performance (or mask) is needed while still retaining the freedom to select an appropriate device. In his book *Design with Climate*, Olgyay has suggested the following four steps for designing and examining shading devices:

46

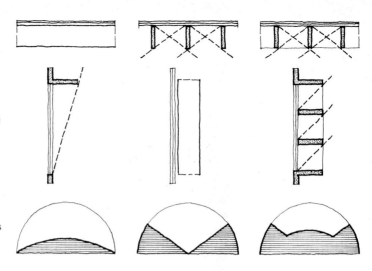

(Far left) A visual explanation of solar angles

(Left) These diagrams show how light at the point of observation will cast a shadow of an object on the sky vault (a) or, conversely, the area from which the observation point will be in shadow if the sun's rays were to come from that portion of the sky vault

(Right) Plans and sections of the basic shading devices with their typical masks

Step 1: The times when shading is needed (the overheated period) must be determined.

Step 2: The position of the sun, during the period when shading is needed, must be determined by using a sun-path diagram.

Step 3: Determine the type and position of the shading device for the overheated period. This is plotted on a protractor having the same scale as the sun-path diagram. The shading masks are independent of latitude, orientation and time, and can be used in any situation. Most shading devices produce shading masks which can be simply resolved into one of three basic types: vertical, where the characteristic shape is bounded by radial lines; horizontal, with a mask of segmental shape, and egg-crate types, which are a combination of the first two.

Step 4: The shading device must be evaluated and its dimensions must be determined to ensure correct shading during the overheated period and to allow, if necessary, some sun to penetrate during the underheated period.

As has already been explained, steps 3 and 4 can be reversed; the required shading can be determined and an appropriate shading device then developed to suit the situation.

(Right) Shady narrow street

(Below left) Canvas awnings provide shade for marketplace in Taxco, Mexico

(Below right) Arcaded sidewalk provides protection from burning sun and from the glare

A number of shading
devices in a small area on
Mykonos; narrow street,
trees, creepers, awnings,
overhanging balconies
and shutters

(Below) Closely grouped
buildings in hot-dry
climate and open, loose
planning in warm-humid
regions

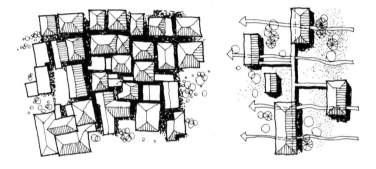

In the hot areas of the world, people are used to spending a great deal of their time outdoors and as this is only possible when external spaces are shaded, the creation of comforatable conditions around and between buildings is extremely important. In hot-dry climates buildings are normally grouped close together to give some shade to each other and to provide shady narrow streets and small spaces between. The tendency in these areas is to make use of arcades, colonnades, and small enclosed courtyards; even larger public open spaces are enclosed, inward looking and shaded for most of the day.

Shade is equally important in the warm-wet zones, but in this case it must be combined with protection from the frequent and often intensive rains while simultaneously allowing free passage for air movement. As vertical elements tend to restrict air flow, screening must be more open than in the arid areas; roof overhangs, verandahs, awnings, pergolas. Most welcome of all is the shade of a tree and the inclusion of shade trees in open-air living spaces and public spaces should have high priority.

49

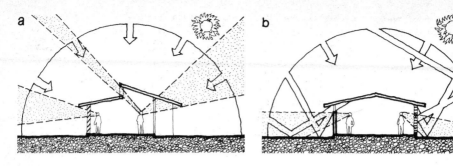

a   b

Glare and daylight

One of the problems in hot climates is to exclude not only radiant heat but also glare, while at the same time admitting sufficient daylight. In this respect, as in many others, there is a fundamental difference between the problem in the arid and humid regions.

In the arid areas glare arises mainly through sunlight being reflected from the surface of the ground and light coloured walls of other buildings. A traditional way of overcoming this problem is by keeping windows on external elevations small and few in number, with the larger, low level windows overlooking the shaded internal courtyard. When small windows are used on the external walls, care must be taken in their design and location to ensure that the problem of glare is not exaggerated by too sharp a contrast between the bright opening and the surrounding inside wall surface. Traditional methods of overcoming this problem are vertical slit windows—usually in the corners of rooms—windows placed between the ceiling and eye-level, and various forms of lattices, screens or shutters to filter external brightness.

High humidity and typically overcast conditions in the warm-wet regions result in a high proportion of the radiation being

(Above) Glare from sky in hot-humid zones can be overcome by using low overhanging eaves and wooden louvres (a). In hot-dry areas reflected glare from the ground and other surfaces is a problem and small, carefully positioned windows, as well as shutters are used (b)

Four types of window designs used to reduce the glare problem in hot-dry areas

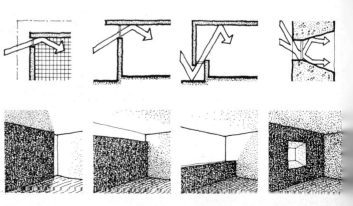

(Right) Three ways of filtering external brightness

(Below) Grills, lattices and side balconies all help to keep out sun and glare in this Australian building

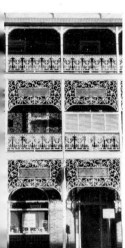

diffused so that the sky, in this case, is the main source of glare which can become almost unbearable. As it is usual to have large openings for cross ventilation, low overhanging eaves or wide verandahs are used to obstruct the view of most of the sky. In traditional houses thin external walls of coarsely woven mats, which can in some cases be rolled up, allow full advantage to be taken of every breeze and admit a good quality of light while completely eliminating glare and providing privacy.

A typical development of the settlers in the hot areas of America, Australia and South Africa was to build a wide verandah on all sides of their houses which provided sitting and sleeping space in an intermediate zone (between indoors and outdoors) even in rainy weather. These verandahs, in addition, shaded the walls and windows, offered protection from glare as well as allowing continuing ventilation during violent storms. This sensible solution had certain disadvantages, however, as interiors tended to be rather gloomy and the sun was eliminated from the interior even during the underheated period of the year. The basic principle of this solution could be used in other ways: for instance, by pergola covered verandahs over which creepers—that lose their leaves in winter—are grown.

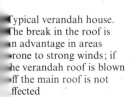

Typical verandah house. The break in the roof is an advantage in areas prone to strong winds; if the verandah roof is blown off the main roof is not affected

Ventilation

Ventilation caused by the stack effect can be a great aid to comfort in humid areas when there is little or no air movement

Natural ventilation and air movement perform three separate functions: the supply of fresh air for health, the cooling of the interior by convection, and the cooling of the inhabitants under certain circumstances. The forces producing natural ventilation in buildings result from air changes caused by differences in temperature—the so-called 'stack effect' where warmer and lighter indoor air is displaced by cooler and denser outdoor air—and by air movement or flow produced by pressure differences. Whereas the movement of air at a relatively slow pace, as a result of thermal forces (the stack effect), may be adequate for both the supply of fresh air and convection cooling, these forces are rarely sufficient to create the appreciable air movements required in some hot zones to provide thermal comfort. The only natural force which can be relied on for this purpose is the dynamic effect of winds and every effort must be made to capture as much wind as possible.

Indoor air flow is affected by various factors, including the following:

Orientation

Unfortunately, good solar orientation and that most suitable for the prevailing wind very seldom coincide and the best compromise must be reached in each case. Although the greatest pressure on the windward side of a building is generated when the façade is perpendicular to the wind direction, Givoni has shown that if windows are positioned at 45° to the wind direction, the average indoor air velocity is increased and a better distribution of indoor air movement is provided. This approach may help resolve orientation problems when the solar and wind requirements are contradictory.

Vegetation

And other external features have little or no influence in the control of air movement around high structures, but their position and size can, as has already been explained, have a

(Above) Outline of air flow at 90° (**a**) and 45° (**b**). In the second case the suction effect is increased and indoor air flow improved

Air flow patterns are influenced by vegetation and can be modified by landscaping (**a** and **b**). Hot air should, ideally, be cooled by passing over and through vegetation before entering a building (**c**)

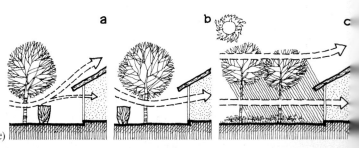

52

marked effect on the movement of air over and around low buildings. By day, in warm-humid areas where ventilation is so important, the air should enter the building through shade without passing over or through heated surfaces and vegetation can play an important role in this respect, as long as it does not restrict the free flow of the breeze.

Cross ventilation

As wind blows against a structure air piles up on the windward side, creating an area of high pressure. With the air flowing around the building an area of reduced pressure is created directly downwind of the structure. Thus a pressure difference exists between the windward and leeward side in such a way that air will move through the structure—if adequate openings exist—from the high pressure side (or pressure zone) to the low pressure side (or suction zone).

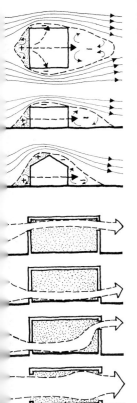

The larger the windows, the higher will be the indoor air speeds, but this is true only when the inlet and outlet openings are increased simultaneously. When a room has unequal openings and the outlet is the larger, then much higher maximum velocities and slightly higher average speeds are obtained. Care must be taken not to impede cross ventilation with incorrectly designed interior partitions, and to ensure effective air movement by correct positioning and sizes of openings. When a room is divided by means of a partition—or several rooms occur together with inlets and outlets separated by doors or halls—the air changes direction and speed as it passes through the room. This, in general, reduces air movement, although by creating a turbulent, circulating movement of air within the room it may result in effective ventilation of more of the area. Satisfactory ventilation is possible in buildings when air has to pass from one room to another, as long as the connection between the spaces remains open when the ventilation is required. As velocities are lowest when the partition is close to the inlet window—it forces the air to change direction rapidly—

(Above) Basic air flow patterns through rooms for various sizes and positions of openings

When inlet is larger than outlet velocity of air flow is increased outside the room (a); to increase velocity inside, inlet must be smaller than outlet (b). Position of internal pattern affects air flow pattern (c and d)

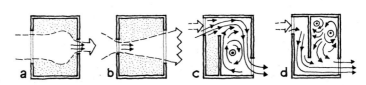

a b c d

In the humid tropics it is important to ensure that air flows into a room at a level which suits its function (**a**). Louvres can deflect the air flow upwards or downwards (**b** and **c**). A canopy over a window tends to direct air flow upwards (**d**) and a gap between it and the wall ensures a downward pressure (**e**) which is further improved in the case of a louvred sunshade (**f**)

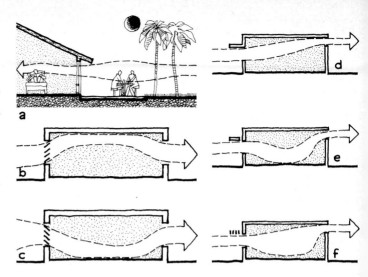

it is preferable for the larger rooms on the prevailing upwind side to maximise air movements within the complex.

Although the aim should be to encourage air movement throughout the full depth of rooms—floor to ceiling—and it is important to ensure that air flows into the space at a level, and in a pattern, which suits its function. For instance in bedrooms, particularly in warm-humid zones, the main air flow should be in that part of the room where beds are located and at a height a little above bed level.

The indoor air-flow pattern is influenced mainly by the position and design of the inlet openings and is also affected by overhangs and sun-shading devices. The direction of flow within the room can be controlled by the type of opening sections provided in windows, and by the use of adjustable louvres and shutters. If the sashes of horizontal centre-pivot-hung windows can be made to open downwards to 10° below the horizontal on the room side they, as well as adjustable louvres, are the most suitable for directing the incoming air to any desired level within the room.

Movement of air from outside to inside a building may be both desirable and undesirable depending on its temperature in relation to the interior temperature. In hot regions, if the air temperature is below the temperature in the building or below

Wind patterns are altered by the layout of groups of buildings, and wind *shadows* as well as flows in an opposite direction to the wind can be created (see text)

(Below) The extent of the wind *shadow* increases in proportion to the height of a building and is affected by the roof pitch. The width of the building has little effect on the extent of the *shadow*

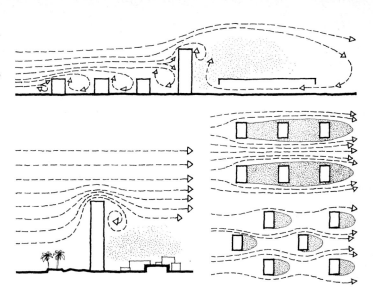

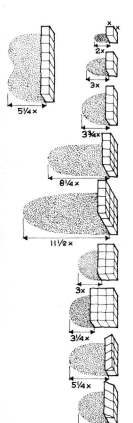

body temperature, air flow is encouraged in order to promote cooling by evaporation and a feeling of comfort with air movement. The floors of the traditional airy pavilion-like houses in warm-wet regions are sometimes raised on stilts for better exposure to prevailing breezes which tend to be damped by the surrounding vegetation. In addition, this method of construction enables cooling of the floor from below— particularly beneficial at night—as well as protecting the building from floods and various insects and rodents. In hot-dry climates, especially if the air temperature is near or above body temperature, reduction of day-time ventilation to a minimum is necessary to prevent additional heating of the interior. Ventilation is only desirable during the night-time period, to reduce the indoor air temperature and to offset the effect of the heat being radiated from the warm internal surfaces.

In a warm climate provision for air movement must be a major consideration in deciding on the layout of groups or clusters of buildings. The effect of tall buildings must be analysed and it must be kept in mind that if a low building is situated in the wind shadow of a high block, this can result in the air flowing through the low building in a direction opposite to that of the wind. To obtain a more uniform flow of air in cluster schemes, it is advisable to use a checker-board lay-out with the buildings staggered rather than to lay them out in rigid rows.

Aids for cooling

Wind catchers

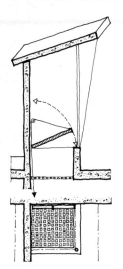

The inlet to the wind tower can usually be closed to keep out dust or cold air. Screens are often provided to keep out insects and birds

Or wind towers can be found in hot climate areas ranging from Pakistan through the Gulf States to Egypt and North Africa, and although the form and details may vary from region to region, the basic principle of catching unobstructed higher level breezes, remains the same. In some places the catchers are unidirectional and orientated to catch the favourable breezes, while in other places pivoted scoops and multi-directional towers utilise winds from any direction. In the oriental courtyard houses of Iraq, for example, a series of wind catchers on the roof provide natural ventilation for a basement room where the residents normally take their summer afternoon siesta. Each catcher is connected to the basement by a duct contained between the two skins of a party wall which is cooled during the night by natural through ventilation. Because it does not receive any direct solar radiation and because of its thickness, the surfaces of the internal party wall remain at a lower temperature than the rest of the interior throughout the day. The incoming air is cooled by conduction when it comes into contact with the cold inner surfaces of the duct walls and its relative humidity is increased as it passes over porous water jugs just before being discharged into the basement. After passing through the basement the air flows into the courtyard, helping to ventilate this area during the daytime.

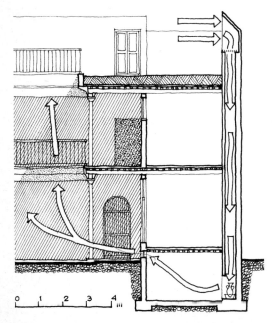

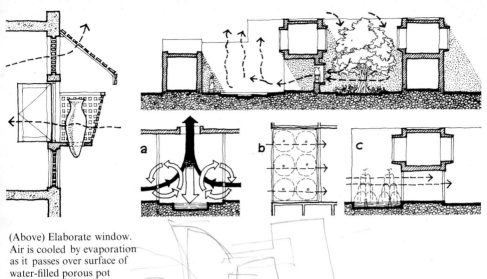

(Above) Elaborate window. Air is cooled by evaporation as it passes over surface of water-filled porous pot

Evaporative coolers

(Top right) Two-courtyard house. Air from shaded courtyard flows over evaporative coolers to larger warm courtyard. Inhabitants spend hottest hours of summer days in the cooled space between the courtyards

A courtyard pool has a beneficial effect at night as well as during the day. Relay of heat to outside aids convection movement and causes air to be drawn through surrounding rooms (**a**). Air passing over water sprays before entering a building is cooled and cleaned (**b** and **c**)

(Far left) The wind catchers in the oriental courtyard houses of Iraq (see also p. 39)

(left) Wind towers in the Bastakia district of Dubai

Warm air passing over water evaporates the water and, as a significant amount of heat is absorbed in the process, the air is cooled. The evaporated water is retained in the air thus increasing its humidity; for this reason evaporative coolers can only be used in relatively dry climates and are found in desert, composite and Mediterranean zones. These coolers are based on the evaporation of a thin film of water on a carrier over or through which air is passed. The simplest system is a wooden frame across which open weave matting of vegetable fibre is stretched. When hung in front of windows in the path of the natural air flow, and kept damp, the matting humidifies and cools the air as well as filtering out the dust. Another simple system entails the use of large, porous earthernware pots filled with water which seeps through the walls of the pot moistening the outside and cooling the passing air as it evaporates. In wind catchers, beds of wet charcoal over which the air passes before entering the room, are sometimes used.

The same principle can be used by channelling breezes over pools or water sprays before they enter buildings. To ensure that the cooled and humidified air enters the building, the pool should be contained between walls on two or, preferably, three sides. A spray pond is more effective than a still pool of the same size and has the additional advantage that is not only cools the air but can also 'wash' it: the water droplets stick to dust particles in the air which can then no longer remain in suspension.

Warm-humid zones

Climate and summary of characteristics	High rainfall and high humidity are associated with a low diurnal range and a relatively high and even temperature throughout the year. Light winds and long periods of still air. Radiation intensity high; large proportion diffused so strong sky glare. Rain usually in afternoon often accompanied by violent electric storms.
Problems and requirements	Uncomfortably hot, sticky conditions which require high air velocity past the body to increase efficiency of sweat evaporation throughout the year. The dominant characteristics required of buildings are openness and shading: they must be designed to provide continuous and efficient ventilation, and protection from sun, rain and insects. Structures may need to withstand hurricane velocity winds and in certain cases safe shelters may be necessary for the hurricane period. Termites can be a problem.
Response: general	Layout and form: buildings separated and scattered with free spaces between them to utilise air flow. Individual structures should be freely elongated; rooms preferably single banked with access from open verandahs or galleries. It may be advantageous to raise buildings on stilts. Orientation: north and south for habitable rooms, but if buildings are in shade variation possible to provide maximum air flow. Orientation to reduce solar radiation most important with high rise buildings. Rooms: should ideally have openings on both the windward and leeward sides. Heat and moisture producing areas should be isolated and separately ventilated. Outdoor areas: as for buildings, they should be shaded; vegetation must not block free passage of air. Adequate storm water drainage must be provided.
Response: structure	Windows and ventilation: openings should be large with inlets of similar size where wide spread of air is needed. Large sliding or folding walls and adjustable louvres commonly used. Screens, lattices, grills etc are useful to admit air flow and provide protection against glare. Flyscreens essential—reduce air flow so best installed away from windows, eg around verandah or balcony. Openings must be protected from radiation, glare, driving rain and noise. Walls: have less thermal value than in any other zone. Lightweight construction of materials with low thermal capacity. If height of walls is kept down it is easier to shade them and protect them from rain. Unshaded walls must be insulated and have a reflective outer surface. Roof: pitched to shed rain and with wide overhang for protection against glare etc. Lightweight, low thermal capacity, ventilated double roof preferable but must be able to withstand strong winds. Reflective roof covering: ceiling well insulated and with reflective upper surface. Space between roof and ceiling well proofed against insects, rodents etc. Surfaces: roof and exposed walls should be reflective (light coloured). It is difficult, however, to maintain light coloured paints in this climate because of high humidity and fungal growth.
Note: Tropical marine	In warm-humid island zones the sun will be lower in sky so greater intensity of solar radiation on wall facing the equator. Extra care needed in protection of this wall. Winds more reliable but hurricanes present a hazard.

58

Hot-dry zones

Climate and summary of characteristics

High intensity of direct solar radiation plus radiation reflected from ground. High diurnal and annual temperate ranges. Low humidity and low precipitation. Sandy environment with dust storms. Climate generally healthier than those of warm-humid lands.

Problems and requirements

Uncomfortable conditions created by extremes of heat and dryness. Flies, sand and dust storms are a nuisance. Buildings must be adapted to summer conditions—basically a problem of protection from intense radiation from sun, ground and surrounding buildings. Reduction of heat takes precedence over air movement during daytime. Measures must be taken to reduce glare and to prevent dust penetration.

Response: general

Layout and form: compact planning for groups of buildings to provide mutual shading and minimum exposure. Enclosed, compactly planned and inward looking buildings most suitable: patios and courtyards advisable. For large buildings high, cubical and massive forms are advantageous. Orientation: larger dimensions and windows should face north and south. Worst orientation, west-east, can be used for non-habitable spaces to form a thermal barrier. _to collect heat._ Rooms: can be deep, should ideally open on to patio or indoor courtyard. Heat producing areas should be isolated and separately ventilated. Outdoor areas: must be enclosed, inward looking, contain plants, be cooled by water and be shaded for most of the day. Paved surfaces should be avoided wherever possible. Provision must be made for outdoor sleeping.

Response: structure

Windows and ventilation: relatively small, particularly on outside walls, and must be shielded from direct radiation and glare. Ventilation during daytime must be kept to the minimum required for hygienic reasons; good ventilation required at night. Walls: simplest solution is to follow tradition and use thickest suitable walls. Rooms used only in evenings can be of materials with low heat-retaining capacity which cool quickly after sunset. Roof: solid and heat storing with a reflective upper surface—flat concrete roofs often used. Water spray or pool on roof can be effective. Double roof sometimes used: lower portion heavy with reflective upper surface, outer layer lightweight with highly reflective surface above and low emittance surface below; ventilated air space between the two layers. Surfaces: whitewash is cheapest, simplest and most effective way of making outer surfaces reflective: needs to be frequently repainted. Can cause glare off walls—light brown colour sometimes used.

Note: Maritime zones

Maritime zones similar but higher humidity causes discomfort; humidity tends to reduce diurnal variations and moderate temperatures. Air movement required at times so high termal capacity structure not as effective. Wind towers very effective in these zones. Ideal to have lightweight area utilising breeze for daytime use.

59

Composite zones

Climate and summary of characteristics

Two or three distinct seasons; one similar to that of hot-dry deserts (usually longest period), another to the warm-wet zones. Some places have a third season, cool and dry with low humidity, warm sunny days and cold nights. Diurnal range large during dry seasons; small during wet period.
Radiation and direction of glare vary with seasons.

Problems and requirements

Complex climates from designer's point of view. Buildings must satisfy conflicting needs of hot-dry and warm-humid periods and must, in some places, make provision for a cool or cold season. Where incompatible needs arise, length, duration and relative severity of seasons must be analysed to find balanced solution and most satisfactory compromise. The Mahoney Tables would be useful for assessing requirements: a study of local building traditions is also helpful.

Response: general

Layout and form: with conflicting requirements different solutions may be equally appropriate. Layout should be moderately compact to provide mutual shading and shelter from wind in cold season but allow advantage to be taken of prevailing breezes in humid period. Courtyard buildings are suitable, terraced buildings facing north and south may also be appropriate.
Orientation: toward north and south but prevailing breezes during humid period must be considered as well as radiation required in cold months.
Rooms: if double banked, adequate internal openings must be provided to ensure good air flow during humid period.
Outdoor spaces: courtyard most pleasant space for most of year if shaded during hot period and sunny during cool months; pergola with deciduous creeper can be solution. Provision for outdoor sleeping may be essential.

Response: structure

Windows and ventilation: medium sized openings in opposite walls but with thick shutters to reduce flow of heat and dusty air during hot, dry season (opened in evenings) and cold air in cool season. Provision must be made for ventilation during these periods; simplest solution one high level and one low level opening. Wind towers are sometimes used with catcher opening covered during cold weather. Windows must be protected from radiation and glare (both from sky and ground) but shading undesirable in winter.
Walls: thick heavy walls are required for hot-dry and cold periods but as large openings are needed in outer walls, thermal capacity should be provided through heavy internal walls, floors and ceilings. In hot seasons walls should be shaded and surfaces exposed to sun should be light coloured. In cold period sun is required on walls.
Roof: heavy with reflective outer surface. Large projecting eaves advisable for shade and protection against glare and rain.
Surfaces: those exposed to the sun during the hot and warm seasons should be light coloured or of shiny metal. Some of the surfaces receiving sun during the cold (but not the hot) season should be absorptive.

Note: Uplands

Upland (or highland) zones, although having more moderate temperatures, are dominated by strong solar radiation; adequate shading for windows and external activities in summer therefore important. Roof very important as it receives greatest amount of radiation. Nights can become cold and some heating may have to be provided for winter.

Sub-tropical: Mediterranean

Climate and summary of characteristics

Summers warm to hot and dry; winters cool to cold with moderate rainfall. Intensive solar radiation especially in summer. Variability of temperatures, humidity and rainfall quite large depending on location, eg marine, continental or mountainous.
Diurnal range: large in continental locations, small in marine locations.

Problems and requirements

Buildings must be designed to provide protection from summer heat and from cold and rain in winter. In continental locations summer heat and dust create problems similar to those found in hot-dry zones, while in marine locations heat and humidity in summer require good ventilation. Condensation can be a problem in winter in marine locations. Dust can be a problem in summer, particularly in continental areas. Some heating in winter is usually necessary.

Response: general

Layout and form: in continental areas the requirements are similar to those in hot dry lands but as climate is more moderate, spacing need not be quite so compact to allow for sun and light in winter. Courtyard plans suitable. In marine areas buildings on east-west axis with adequate spacing to allow for breeze penetration will be more appropriate.
Orientation: because of high intensity of solar radiation, windows should face north and south, but prevailing breezes must be considered in marine locations.
Rooms: preferably single banked in marine areas; if double banked adequate provision must be made for good through air flow.
Outdoor spaces: courtyards for shade in summer and protection from cold winds in winter in continental locations. Shaded areas utilising breeze in marine areas, but protection against winter winds must be kept in mind.

Response: structure

Windows and ventilation: in continental areas the requirements are similar to those in hot-dry lands but with cold winters sun would be welcome during this period. Medium sized openings are needed to ensure good air flow during summer and permit the penetration of sun in winter.
Walls: continental areas, as for hot-dry zones. In marine areas heat capacity is not as important but internal walls and floors could be heavy to store heat during winter while preventing the internal temperature from rising too much when sun is allowed to penetrate through windows.
Roof: sloping roof to shed rain; should provide shade for windows and protection from rain. Otherwise as for hot-dry zones.
Surfaces: wall and roof should be reflective (light coloured) where not shaded.

Note: sub-tropical humid

Complex climate from the designer's point of view. Basically as for warm-humid zones, but provision must be made for the winter months which can be cold. Mahoney Tables would be useful for assessing basic requirements, which will obviously involve some compromise.

61

Chapter 3

Regional hazards

The performance of a building may be greatly influenced by more extreme climatic and environmental factors which vary from place to place. The following hazards can cause damage to a building or result in defects and failures, and therefore require special consideration during the design stage. Some of the hazards can cause disasters on a large scale and the special precautions which must be taken when laying out groups of buildings are also discussed.

Condensation

Condensation occurs mainly under cold conditions and it is possible in any climate where winter heating is needed. It is hardly necessary to discuss here the factors contributing to the formation of condensation under these circumstances nor the measures which must be taken to prevent it, as they are well known to architects working in temperate climates. There are, however, conditions under which condensation may occur in warm-humid and composite climates although it is not as serious a problem.

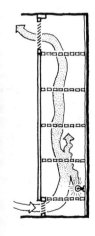

When the temperature drops at night in warm-humid areas it is likely that the air temperature will be lower than that of the internal wall surfaces and it is therefore possible for small amounts of moisture to be deposited on them, causing the dampness which is so characteristic of this climate. This problem can be minimised only by effective and well distributed ventilation which is particularly important in spaces like cupboards, where mould growth can develop quickly in unventilated, warm damp conditions. When once established, the mould can exist under a wide range of temperatures and humidity conditions, but generally it would seem that for active growth the moulds prefer temperatures between 10°C and 21°C and a fairly high relative humidity—usually above 75 per cent. Many of the mould types prefer dark conditions and little air movement. Cupboards and other storage areas should, therefore, open completely and dark inaccessible corners must be avoided. These spaces must be well ventilated with vents at bottom and top—or with louvred doors—and with slatted shelves. When conditions are particularly bad it is common practice to install some form of low-intensity heating, such as a low-wattage light-bulb, to combat humidity.

(left) Hurricane damage

(above) Cross ventilation cupboards

63

In some places with composite climates condensation may occur on indoor walls at the start of the rainy season when the walls are cooled by the night air and there is a subsequent sudden influx of warm, humid air. Although unpleasant when they do occur, such conditions are experienced for only short periods of each year and the simplest solution is to use plasters and paints which are porous, which absorb moisture as condensation occurs and release it again as soon as the air is sufficiently dry. Special paints incorporating fungicides can be used but they will not, however, prevent mould growth on dirt and grease spots, and some of them may lose their fungicidal qualities after a time.

Hail

In some parts of the hot climate zones hail storms occur fairly frequently and although the hail is usually too small to cause much damage, there are occasional freak storms with very large hailstones that can penetrate a light structure. Parts of southern Africa and of Iran are among the areas where such storms are recorded.

When a building is being designed for a site within a known hailbelt, certain precautions should be taken; the roof covering should be hail resistant, overhangs should be sufficient to protect windows, and gutters, which can be blocked by a heavy fall of small hailstones, should be protected with a wire mesh covering. Toughened (heat treated) glass, which has a high resistance to hail damage and does not normally require additional protection, can be used in windows not adequately protected. Where normal glass is used and where water penetration—rain entering through windows broken by hail—would cause serious damage or loss, it may be advisable to protect windows with hail guards which can consist of a light framework covered with 16 mm square mesh of 14 gauge wire. It would be desirable to protect the glass of solar water heaters with a similar screen (see section on solar energy further on).

Lightning

Lightning, which is the result of discharge of accumulated static electricity between cloud and cloud or cloud and earth, can cause a great deal of costly damage when it is of the latter type. As thunderstorms, often accompanied by violent air to ground lightning, are fairly common in many parts of the hot climate areas, it is important that in these places adequate steps are taken to protect buildings.

The danger of lightning is twofold:

Heat   If any material containing moisture is subjected to the tremendous heat generated by a lightning flash (temperatures can reach 20000°C and more), the instantaneous expansion of the moisture to vapour results in an explosion—something which can be clearly seen when a tree is struck by lightning. Although the moisture content of concrete or brick and mortar in buildings is considerably less, the mechanism is the same.

Side flash   Or the passage of electricity from one point to another through an intervening space. If lightning strikes an object and cannot dissipate its energy to earth, it will flash to any adjacent metal structure—up to a distance of approximately 15 m—in an attempt to do this. Side flash is common in buildings with unsatisfactory earthing, particularly if they have metal roofs or metal structures such as aerials and air conditioning units on the roofs. Window panes on high-rise buildings are another cause of this phenomenon.

There is no way to prevent or arrest lightning and the best defence for buildings which are prone to strikes by virtue of their position or height is a well designed protection system which, if struck, will conduct the charge safely to ground and adequately dissipate it. Any protection system will consist of two basic parts—earthing (or earth electrode) and the conductor itself (also called a collector or air termination), which is sometimes connected to the earthing by a separate down conductor.

Lightning conductor   The part of a protection system that is intended to intercept the lightning discharge and which may consist of a mast erected in close proximity to the building to be protected, a metallic roof, or a roof conductor (horizontal or vertical) fastened to a non-metallic roof. The zone of protection provided is cone-shaped in the case of a vertical conductor and wedge-shaped in the case of a horizontal one. The protective angle of a single conductor is normally 45° but in a situation of high risk—when a building is over 30 m high or is on or near the top of a hill—it is only 30°.

Masts or poles, usually of steel or aluminium tubes, are probably the most effective but most expensive conductors. As a single mast would have to be very high to protect all parts of a

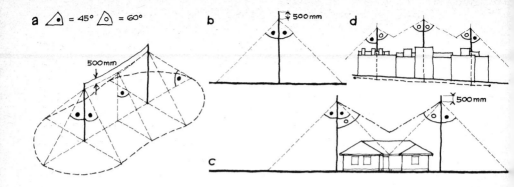

Zones of protection with different forms of conductors. Two vertical masts with a horizontal conductor between them (**a**); a single mast (**b**); double masts (**c**) and a series of vertical spikes (**d**)

building, they are normally used in pairs (one at each end of the building) or in conjunction with one or more spikes (vertical roof conductors). The mast should be erected as close as possible to the building, but must be at least 1 m away from the eaves or outside walls. No down conductor is required and the lower end of the mast is connected to a terminal on the earthing, approximately 0·3 m above the ground level. Stay wires used to support a mast must be earthed at their anchor points.

Roof conductors, spikes and down conductors: strip, rod, tube or stranded wire of copper, brass, aluminium, galvanised steel or stainless steel can be used for these conductors and they should, in all cases, have a cross sectional area of at least 30 mm². When horizontal roof conductors are used it is preferable to lay them in such a way that two paths are provided for the current to flow along to the earthing. Lightning conductors in the form of spokes, horizontal roof conductors or metallic roofs must be connected to the earthing by means of down conductors which take the most direct path and which should be evenly spaced around the perimeter of the building.

On roofs with highly flammable covering such as thatch, reeds or palm-leaves, the roof conductors should be placed on impregnated hardwood or other insulating supports at a height of not less than 300 mm above the roof. These types of roof are found mainly in the warm-humid zones where there is every chance that there will be trees in the vicinity of the building. If so, their branches should be kept at a distance of at least 2 m from the roof to minimise the possibility of a side flash from a tree to the building.

Earthing

Two types of earthing are commonly used: vertical earthing or earth rods, and horizontal or trench earthing. Vertical earthing usually consists of copper (in soft ground only), copper-coated steel, galvanised steel or stainless steel in the form of rods (16 mm diameter) or thick-walled pipes (20 mm diameter) driven approximately 1·5 m into the ground. The upper end of the earth rod is left protruding above the ground to enable the down conductor to be connected to it. Solid conductors of the same metals can be used for trench earthing and should have a cross-sectional area of at least 35 mm². Alternatively, galvanised steel pipe (25 mm diameter), with the open ends blanked off, may be used. This form of earthing is laid in trenches 0·5 m deep and surrounded with soil.

Ground conditions permitting, earth rods are better to use. They are cheaper and easier to install and it is less likely that the resistivity of the surrounding earth will be affected by seasonal moisture variations. The most effective form of trench earthing is one which surrounds the structure as a closed ring or loop which should be at least 1–2 m from the building. Alternatively, where the outer walls of a building rest on a concrete foundation, a conductor (usually of galvanised steel) embedded in the concrete can be used as an earth electrode. This type of foundation earth is relatively cheap to install and has the great advantage of being free from corrosion. Where foundations are reinforced, the reinforcing bars themselves can be used as earthing provided that they are effectively bonded together and are provided with connections for the down conductors.

High-rise structures (including those constructed of reinforced concrete) are particularly prone to being struck by lightning and, as the upper third of the building usually falls outside the protective zone of any conductors, metal window frames and other metallic parts in this section should be bonded to the down conductors of the lightning protection system. Down conductors can be a problem on very high buildings and one way to overcome some difficulties (for example aesthetic ones) in concrete structures is to use the reinforcing bars which must, of course, be connected together by clamps, welding or by binding wire to ensure electrical continuity. It should perhaps be made clear that it is not necessary to bond all the steel reinforcing in the building, but only that reinforcement which is to be used as a route for down conduction. The more bars there are contributing to the current distribution, however, the better will be the overall protection offered by the system. In buildings

Trench earthing of a mast with as many 80 m lengths as required and a ring earth

Parapet and down conductors on a large building. The windows, balconies and handrails of the top third of the structure should be bonded into the protection system. Thin stipple line indicates the zone of protection

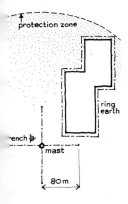

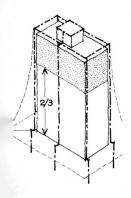

67

constructed of prefabricated reinforced concrete components a down conductor can be formed by connecting some of the reinforcing bars in the precast panels with flexible links.

Not only is it important to safeguard the building against fire and structural damage but also the internal components— particularly its electrical installations and apparatus—must be protected. Electrical breakdown due to excessive potential differences inside a structure and in electrical installations has to be prevented and the magnitude of induced voltages in electrical systems has to be limited to safe values. This latter aspect has become particularly important for electronic systems (computers among other things), the operating voltages and the insulation levels of which are very low. A description of how equalisation of potentials should be effected for all metallic installations—all types of pipes, metal components on and in the structure, and electrical systems—is given in Volume 2 of the book, *Lightning*, edited by R. H. Golde (see Bibliography).

Insects

The nuisances caused by flies, mosquitoes and other insects is a problem in most of the hot climate zones; a problem which is most noticeable on hot evenings when windows must be open to catch any cool breezes, and hundreds of insects are attracted to the indoor lights. Although there is no perfect protection against this problem, it is advisable (and often essential) to provide fly-screens on outside openings in many of the areas under discussion.

The problem in most warm-humid areas, where fly-screens are essential, is that these screens have the disadvantage of reducing the air speeds which are so important for relieving discomfort. Smooth nylon net, which is more durable than the metal mesh which tends to corrode, has the additional advantage of having a lower reducing factor (approximately 35 per cent) than other materials used for this purpose. The best way of minimising the air flow problem is to mount the screen away from the opening and allow it to extend over a much larger area. Where balconies or verandahs are available, the screening should, ideally, run around the perimeter of such areas. Screens to outside door must, if they are to be effective, be self-closing. Where the problem of mosquitoes, flies and other insects is only seasonal the frames carrying the mesh can be opened or removed during the period they are not required.

68

In addition to providing screening, the insect nuisance can be reduced by cutting back undergrowth near buildings; ensuring that there is no standing water near the buildings or in gutters etc; and by using a few external lights to divert mosquitoes and other insects away from windows and doors.

Termites

There are about 1900 known species of termites distributed throughout the tropics, some hundred of which can be connected with damage to buildings. Of this group over 50 species constitute a serious threat causing considerable damage to wood and cellulose based materials used in buildings. There are two main types of termites which must be considered.

Drywood termites

Or the wood-inhabiting species (belonging mainly to the family Calotermitidae) which differ from all other species infesting buildings in that their colonies inhabit and complete their life cycle entirely within dry timber, no contact with the soil being needed. The feeding habits of and proofing measures against these species closely correspond to those of the wood-boring beetles, and like the beetles they may fly into buildings or be introduced in previously infested timber. As this type generally requires a fairly high relative humidity, it is most often found in coastal and damp inland areas.

Subterranean termites

Which can be divided into two sub-groups—Those not destroying wood (eg some species of the family Hodotermit-idae). This type frequently infests buildings and although never attacking timber has a considerable nuisance value undermining walls with their tunnels and destroying wallpaper, cotton, curtaining, clothes, books, thatch and other similar materials containing cellulose. Protective measures designed to exclude entry of subterranean wood-destroying termites would also exclude these species, but as they never attack wood, preservative treatment of structural timber is unnecessary where they alone have to be considered.

Those destroying wood (eg species of the families Rhinotermit-idae and Termitidae). The species of the family Rhinotermit-idae normally nest below the surface out of doors. Some, however, frequently nest in hollows within tree trunks maintaining contact with the soil by means of passages within the trunks or, more frequently, through covered runways along the outside. In exceptional cases they may nest out of contact with the soil in buildings, but then only when a constant source of moisture is available there.

A widely differing range of nesting and feeding habits can be found among the species of the family Termitidae. Some nest mainly in surface mounds, while others place their nests well below the soil surface and the absence of any conspicuous mounds can result in buildings being erected over active colonies. Some species do not readily adapt their nesting and feeding habits to conditions prevailing within buildings, but there are others that adapt with ease and would even seem to prefer this unnatural environment.

The full procedure which is recommended for preventing damage by subterranean termites in buildings is set out fully in various publications and only a broad outline is given here.

The site
A careful examination must be made for surface signs of subterranean nests, and trees in the vicinity must be scrutinised for the tell-tale runways against the trunks. All nests on or near the site must be destroyed—usually by application of suitable toxic smokes forced into the nest system under pressure or by treatment with liquid fumigants.

Foundations
All roots and other cellulose matter which might provide food for termites must be removed from under the building. Every effort must be made to keep the ground underneath the building as dry as possible by providing adequate and effective drainage for surface waters. To prevent the access of termites through the foundations, concrete in the footings should be well consolidated and free from honeycombing and all brickwork below floor level should be grouted up solid.

Poisoning
Whatever form of construction is used, it is essential to poison the soil beneath the building; this repels or exterminates termites attempting to pass through the poisoned soil layer. Pentachlorephenol, sodium pentachlorophenate, dieldrin, aldrin and chlordane are poisons commonly used. The solution is applied by flooding it on to the levelled soil below a suspended floor or the consolidated filling below a solid floor. It is also

usual to treat the ground around both sides of the foundation walls by pouring the poisoned solution into trenches dug for this purpose.

Ground floor

In the case of a concrete slab laid on the ground over hardcore and filling, care must be taken to ensure that there will be no open cracks; a crack of 1 mm is sufficient to allow the passage of a termite. In the case of a floating slab it may be advisable to use V-shaped expansion joints at regular intervals. The joints should be filled with poison solution which must be allowed to soak away before being sealed with a pitch compound. The joint between the floor slab and surrounding walls should be treated in the same way.

Where suspended floors are used adequate ventilation of the sub-floor area is essential and access to this space must be provided. Sheet metal termite shields are often fitted to the top of the foundation and to sleeper walls and piers, but do not always provide adequate protection, as some species are able to contact suspended floors by means of moundlike structures. Regular inspection of the sub-floor area is therefore important.

Soil under floor and around foundation walls must be poisoned, and the joint between slab and wall sealed with a bituminous compound (a). Adequate ventilation of sub-floor area must be provided where suspended floors are used and termite shields may be useful (b). These do not always provide adequate protection as some termites build moundlike nests (c)

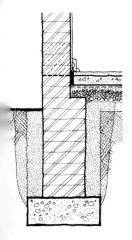

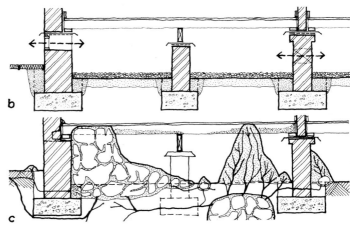

b

c

Drainage	The ground underneath the building must be kept as dry as possible by providing effective drainage away from the building for surface waters and ensuring that there is no possibility of leakage from plumbing.
Timber	Preservative treatment, at least for structural timber, will usually be necessary to ensure the highest degree of protection and to provide a safeguard against drywood termites and wood-boring beetles.

Sand and dust

Many of the drier hot areas suffer from the considerable nuisance of sand and dust, which apart from causing physical discomfort—irritation to the eyes, nose and throat—also cause a great deal of extra cleaning work and they can, furthermore, have a detrimental effect on building materials. A continual bombardment by wind-blown sand is often the cause of damage to wood, metals, paints, galvanising and other exterior surfaces, while sand collecting in roof spaces not only adds considerably to the structural loading, but also reduces the efficiency of a double roof.

Saini (*Building Environment*, see Bibliography) describes the characteristics of dust and sand movement in hot-dry lands fairly fully and explains that the important difference is that while sand drifts along the ground—never much more than 1 m above the surface even in strong winds—the smaller dust particles can be lifted to a considerable height and are carried for long distances before returning to the ground.

A square central courtyard offers good protection from windblown dust and sand (**a**). The depth of a rectangular courtyard should not exceed 3A unless the long axis is perpendicular to the wind (**b**). The same holds true for perimeter courtyards (**c**). Barrier screens must be of a suitable height and not more than 6 m from the building to provide protection (**d–f**)

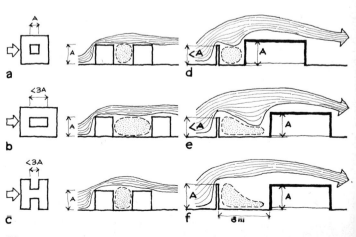

72

Sand, because of its tendency to bounce along the ground, can be effectively stopped by relatively small barrier screens—about 1·7 m high—while inner courtyards are obviously advantageous for overcoming this nuisance. The penetration of dust, however, is rather more difficult to control and barriers, which need to be at least as high as the building itself and not more than 6 m away from the façade if they are to provide adequate protection, will tend to exclude the possibility of utilising fully the cool evening breezes. An inner courtyard can also give protection from most of the wind-borne dust if its depth, relative to the direction of the prevailing wind, is not more than twice the height of the building.

Shutters, which can be closed as required, are probably the simplest way of obtaining a large measure of protection from both sand and dust on the pressure side of buildings, while most of the methods utilised to combat solar radiation—vegetation, small openings in façades, closely built structures and narrow winding streets—all help to reduce considerably the problem of wind-blown sand and dust.

Tropical storms

While some provision must normally be made in building design for wind forces, much greater care must be given to this aspect in areas subject to tropical storms, and in places where squalls of very strong wind are common, even if they are of short duration only. These violent storms which have a variety of names according to the region in which they occur—hurricanes, typhoons, and cyclones—are all basically the same phenomenon; rotating winds of high speed (120 km per hour or more) which can affect widespread areas over a substantial period. Because of the extensive damage that can be caused by not only the direct effects of wind and excessive rainfall, but also the secondary effects of flooding, storm surge and landslides, these cyclonic storms are potentially one of the most damaging of all natural phenomena.

Tornadoes, although the smallest of all tropical storms and confined to a relatively small geographical area, are the most violent, developing wind velocities of from 160 to 480 km per hour. They have a width of a few hundred metres—compared with the 500 to 600 km average diameter of the cyclonic storms—and while they have been reported to travel up to 300 km, they often peter out after as little as 20 km.

In areas where there is any chance of tropical storms occurring, it is essential for the designer to ascertain whether there are any codes in force (various codes which range from performance types to specification types are in use in the USA, Japan and the Bahamas), as well as to collect all available records of former storms. In addition to reliable meteorological data, case histories and newspaper reports can be most useful. For coastal areas subject to cyclonic storms and which do not have codes the United Nations has proposed a scale which provides some means of comparing the effects of storms of various intensities. In this regard it should be noted that the destructive power of wind increases with the square of its speed, so that a tenfold increase in wind speed increases its force 100 times.

Grade and velocity 2- or 3-second gusts at 9·20 m elevation	Damage
1:120 kmph–150 kmph	To shrubbery, trees and foliage, but not to building structures.
2:151 kmph–180 kmph	Considerable to shrubbery and tree foliage with some trees blown down. Buildings: some damage to roofing materials, windows and doors; no major damage to structures.
3:181 kmph–210 kmph	Extensive damage to trees and shrubs; large trees blown down. Buildings: some damage to roofing materials, doors, windows, curtainwalls and small structures.
4:211 kmph–240 kmph	Shrubs and trees blown down. Buildings: extensive damage to roofing materials, windows and doors; some curtainwall failures. Complete failure of roof structures on many small buildings.
5:241 kmph and over	Shrubs and trees blown down. Buildings: considerable damage to roofs, windows and doors. Complete failure of roof structures on many small buildings. Extensive curtainwall failure and sidewall failure on industrial buildings. Some small buildings overturned.

Traditional Yami house built mostly below ground as protection against typhoons

(Below) The effect of wind force on various forms of roof

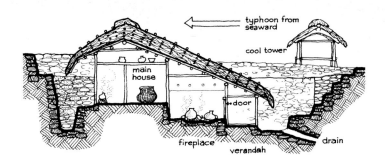

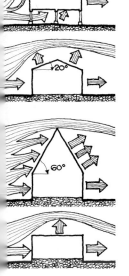

Resistance to lateral forces of winds generally requires either rigidity or bracing, but one solution to the problem commonly used by primitive builders is flexibility: the use of tied joints which allows their structures to sway and give in the winds much like a palm tree. Another method is to virtually avoid the problem altogether by sinking the building below ground level.

A building in cyclonic storm areas must be able to withstand the extreme winds that blow from every direction during the same storm, as well as withstand the rapid and extreme changes in air pressure. Roofs are particularly prone to being destroyed by high suction on their lee side due to the rapid air flow over the building or a combination of suction on top and pressure underneath the large overhangs so common in these areas. The effects of air pressure differences between the windward side and leeward side can also cause severe oscillations and result in failure, in the case of tall structures. The centre of a cyclonic storm is at extremely low pressure and if this hits a building which is particularly well sealed too quickly, the normal pressure inside the building can cause it to explode outward and collapse and it is therefore an advantage for any building not to be too airtight.

The rainfall associated with a tropical storm can be intense over a lengthy period—it can last from 12 to 48 hours and as much as between 75 and 300 mm may fall—and in addition to the problems of flooding and the risk of landslides (these will be discussed in a later section), water can seep into buildings as well as damage foundations and materials. Certain materials and building techniques should be avoided; walls of unburnt earth or wattle and daub, clay mortar, and thatch or leaves in roofing, for example, are all susceptible to severe damage.

75

In addition to considering the wind as a primary load together with the other primary loads (dead loads, live loads etc) when designing a building, the following precautionary measures must also be taken into account:

Siteworks
Buildings can be protected by planting trees not less than 15 m away. In coastal areas, where high tidal surges are likely, buildings should be constructed on earth mounds or raised on stilts (timber poles or concrete columns) so that the floor level of the structure is sufficiently elevated above the high water level.

Foundations
Should be broad so that they can transfer a portion of the forces that arise to the ground.

Structure
Buildings raised on stilts are more liable to uplift and particular care should be taken with their design. In all cases extra strong joints are required between foundations and walls, as well as between walls and floor slabs or roofs, by means of steel reinforcing, bolts, etc. Heavy material should be utilised as far as possible and sufficient diagonal bracing should be provided for stability.

Roofs
All roof elements such as purlins, cladding materials etc should be securely fixed. The use of canopies and overhangs should be

Protection of building in tropical storm areas by raising the ground level and planting trees which should be at least 15 m from the building (a). Provision should be made for tying down the roof (b). The building must be securely tied to the foundation (c); be able to resist sheer forces (d); the roof must be properly anchored (e) and roof and floor must be able to transmit lateral loads to end walls (f)

(Far right) Seismic areas and cyclone zones

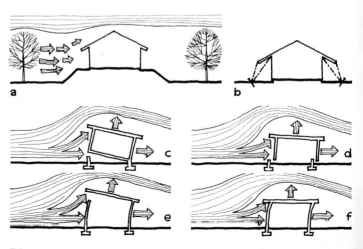

minimised and where this is not possible brackets or hooks, which can be used to tie down the roof before the start of the storm season, should be provided.

Windows   And doors can be a particular source of danger—if they are broken, wind has easy access to the interior and the resultant uplift pressure on the roof can cause the possible destruction of the entire building. Frames should be securely anchored and large glass areas should be protected by shutters.

Earthquakes   Earthquakes are natural phenomena which occur frequently in certain regions of the world, but although the earth's surface is shaken by tremors hundreds of thousands of times each year, relatively few are of an intensity sufficient to cause damage to buildings. The zones of major risk form a belt extending from the American Pacific coast, across Japan, East China, Indonesia and the Middle East to the Mediterranean, and are largely situated in the tropics. Some countries are entirely in seismic areas, while others are divided into three or four probability zones.

Whatever the basic cause, an earthquake usually originates some 5–100 km below the surface of the earth and the place or line where this happens is called the 'focus'. The point on the surface immediately above this is referred to as the epicentre. The sudden rupture at the focus of an earthquake causes

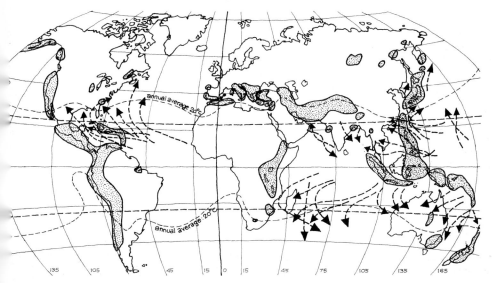

vibrations to go out in all directions in the form of waves which are reflected in different ways by the various materials of the earth's crust causing an unpredictable and complicated pattern. As a result, and in contrast to those types of disaster which affect only one particular location or long strips of area in a uniform way, damage caused by a single earthquake occurs in uneven fashion throughout a region.

As the UNDRO books on *Disaster Prevention and Mitigation* (see Bibliography) explain, earthquakes commonly give rise to a complex chain of events which include surface faulting, ground shaking, and geologic failures (such as ground subsidence, soil liquefaction, landslides and mudflows) and may, furthermore, provoke avalanches and floods. Estimations of earthquake risk are represented in the form of seismic zoning or micro-zoning maps which identify the location and probable intensities of earthquake hazards in a given region or locality. While seismic zoning considers the distribution of earthquake risks over an entire country or region, micro-zoning describes the detailed distribution of risks within the area down to the local and even site level, as ground response may differ from one site to the next, owing to sub-soil and ground surface conditions.

Many scales of intensity have been used and there are still at least three widely in use today. UNESCO, however, has recommended the use of the MSK-64 scale which is divided into 12 degrees of intensity and although differing very little from the other scales at the lower degrees (I–V), it takes the types of construction, the percentage of buildings damaged and the nature of the damage into account from degrees VI–X. A simplified version of the scale, indicating the general effects that may be expected on buildings at the different intensities, is given below.

Classification of the scale

1. Types of struc-   A—cobwork, adobe, rural and ordinary stone buildings
   tures: B—brick, concrete block, half timbered, bonded stonework
                     C—reinforced concrete and strong wooden buildings

2. Percentage of   Q (a few)—about 5 per cent
   buildings damaged: N (many)—about 50 per cent
                     P (most)—75 per cent or more

78

3. Classification of damage:

Grade 1—Slight damage, cracking, fall of debris and plaster.

Grade 2—Moderate damage: cracking of walls, fall of roof tiles, cracking and fall of parts of chimneys.

Grade 3—Heavy damage: large and deep cracks in walls, fall of chimneys.

Grade 4 Destruction: gaps in walls, partial collapse of buildings, internal and infill walls collapse.

Grade 5—Total damage: total collapse of buildings.

Table showing effect on buildings based on above classification

Intensity	Type A			Type B			Type C		
	Q	N	P	Q	N	P	Q	N	P
VI—Strong	2	1		1					
VII—Very strong	4	3		2				1	
VIII—Destructive	5	4		4	3		3	2	
IX—Partially annihilating		5		5	4		4	3	
X—Annihilating			5		5		5	4	

At intensity XI there is severe damage to even well constructed buildings and there is serious ground deformation as well as numerous landslides and rockfalls. At intensity XII practically all structures above and below ground are greatly damaged and destroyed and the whole landscape changes.

In zones where occurrence of earthquakes or tremors is highly probable, buildings must be capable of resisting the stresses caused by the earth waves; horizontal forces as well as resonance phenomena that can occur between the individual vibrations of the building and the vibration frequency of the ground which depends on its surface strata and, more particularly, the local geological characteristics. In addition to the amplification effects of local soil conditions, shaking at a particular site will depend on the distance from the earthquake source and the proximity to the fault line. Experience has shown that the intensity of ground shaking can be much greater on loosely compacted soils than on sites resting on solid bedrock, and a method of assessing potential damage in a given location is to relate the fundamental period of resonance of the projected building or buildings to that of the soil on which they are to stand. When the natural vibration frequency of the building coincides with that of the soil at the foundations, the building will vibrate like a tuning fork when the earthquake hits and shake itself to pieces. Tall buildings, which have long resonance periods, are extremely vulnerable on loose soils whereas one- or two-storey buildings, with shorter periods, are at greater risk on firm ground or bedrock.

There is no standard earthquake code, and even the formula for calculating the forces involved varies from country to country; comprehensive information on this is given in the BRE publication, *Building in Earthquake Areas*, and the various United Nations publications listed in the Bibliography. These publications also describe the basic rules which must be complied with in the design of buildings; they can be summarised as follows:

Form
There is no one ideal form but buildings should be of simple, symmetrical shapes and should not be too elongated in plan or elevation. Round or rectangular buildings are recommended and where L, T or U shapes are used these should be divided into separate units. Avoid: tall narrow buildings.

Foundations
The site must be surveyed to ensure that footings do not span different types of ground. All footings should be at a uniform depth even on sloping ground, and tied together with continuous steel reinforcing. It is recommended that parts of building foundations which rest on soils of different types or are sunk to different depths should be designed as separate units the division must continue through the superstructure. Rubber foundations—which would isolate the building from the shaking—may be a solution and experiments with this possible form of construction are presently being conducted.
Avoid: walls off centre on footings.

Structure
To avoid the torsional effects of earthquake loads the structure should be symmetrical in both plan and elevation—load bearing members should be uniformly distributed—and form a rigid unit. The greater the height of the building the more important this becomes. If parts of a building are of substantially different heights then each will have a different vibration and should, therefore, be structurally independent

80

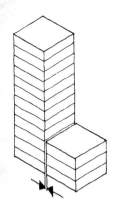

Under dynamic loads, such as those caused by an earthquake, the structure's capacity to absorb energy—or in other words its ductility—is a primary factor to be considered. This ductility depends on the type of material used and also on the structural characteristics of the assembly. Concrete framework, with internal and external walls securely fixed to the frame, is suitable for larger buildings as is structural steelwork, as long as a sufficiently ductile grade of steel is used together with ductile design and fabrication of frame members and connections.

In the case of single- or double-storey brick and stone structures, the ratio of the height to the breadth of the building should not be more than 2:3 and the total area of openings in any one wall should not exceed one-third of the total wall area. This type of structure is very sensitive to earthquake loads and the walls tend to rupture through the joints. It is, therefore, important that good lime or lime-cement mortars are used. A continuously reinforced ring beam can be cast over the top of all walls which should be strengthened with horizontal reinforcing. Avoid: unsymmetrical structural elements eg staircases at one end only.

Above) Where buildings have L, T or U shapes and where parts have different heights, the parts should be divided into separate units

Right) Shapes of buildings should be as simple as possible; long buildings, projections and asymmetric elements must be avoided

Far right) The distribution of walls lacks torsional rigidity in plan (a) and lacks symmetry (b). Satisfactory layouts which provide both torsional rigidity and symmetry (c and d). Rigid unit with small windows is good (e) but no bracing and large single opening is bad (f). The vertical shape should also be simple; very slender buildings, differentiations in height, cantilevers and changes in structural stiffness should be avoided

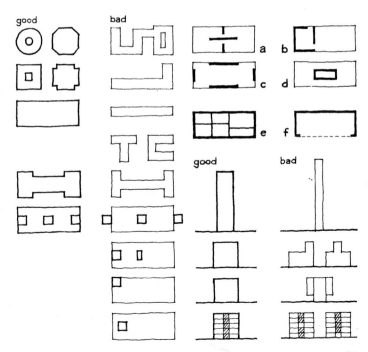

Take care with: large spans which cannot be cross-braced; buildings on pillars which are prone to shear in an earthquake; elements such as overhangs, balconies, parapets, chimneys, roof tanks etc.

Non structural elements

Such as partitions, doors, windows, cladding and finishes are usually supported by the structure and must therefore be able to move with the building without being destroyed. This is particularly true for services and flexibility is required in all pipework to allow for movement of both building and equipment. Infill panels should be designed to cope with the horizontal movements of each floor which are accompanied by vertical deformations changing the clear heights between floors and beams. This can be done by either integrating the infill with the structure or separating it as much as possible. Where rigid walls are integrated with the structure it is usually necessary to reinforce them if seismic deformations are to be satisfactorily withstood. In the case of separated panels the size of the gap, which needs to be between 20–40 mm may make it difficult to obtain lateral stability, sound-proofing and fire-proofing, and suitable flexible materials (which stay permanently soft) may be hard to find.

Avoid: the use of brittle materials; for instance heavy light fittings suspended by brittle supports.

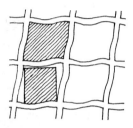

Diagrammatic illustration of differential movement between two storeys as a result of horizontal sway which also causes vertical deformations

Fire

Outbreaks of fire almost always follow a severe earthquake and special precautions must be taken. Structural steelwork must be well protected.

Avoid: the use of any combustible materials near chimneys which may be cracked during a tremor.

Disaster prevention

Tropical storms and earthquakes can, as has already been explained, give rise to chains of events—river flooding, tsunami (tidal waves) and coastal flooding, landslides and fire—which may have disastrous results in human settlements located in zones prone to these occurrences. Many disasters—considered as distinct from the natural phenomena which cause them—can be avoided and physical planning has an important role to play in this regard. Two series of publications dealing with disaster prevention have been published by UNDRO (see Bibliography); the main points which must be considered by designers involved with large-scale projects are summarised here.

82

Densities   In housing developments should not be too high. There is no simple solution to this rule as it may be in conflict with economic criteria or functional demands (for example accessibility and proximity) and a suitable compromise—taking into account local conditions, building technology, height of buildings and so on—must be found for each individual case.

Services   A breakdown in the water supply may be fatal and in any emergency water will be needed for both consumption and fire extinguishing. There should, if possible, be either more than one supply source or an alternative, emergency source; open reservoirs or swimming pools can be used for this purpose and there should be a source of 150–200 m^3 capacity to serve each area of 500 m radius.

Electricity: overhead power lines should be avoided in regions which experience tropical storms. Hospitals, other emergency buildings and the illumination systems of public roadways and footpaths should always have their own emergency supply source.

Gas: the use of gas supply lines in residential areas situated in zones prone to earthquakes is not recommended.

Storm-water: drainage of surface storm-water should not be connected to the sewage system. An emergency network of open ditches, combined with the circulation network, should be provided. In coastal areas with flat topography, dykes or embankments can be built to protect the project from tsunamis and storm surges (as cyclones approach a coastal area, strong on-shore winds can cause a rise of several metres in sea level resulting in flooding of large areas of the interior). Although successive tree lines can help to reduce the force and speed of storm surges, they do not reduce the water level.

Embankment to protect
buildings from storm
surges

Flood protection: care must be taken with the siting of buildings and built-up refuges may have to be provided

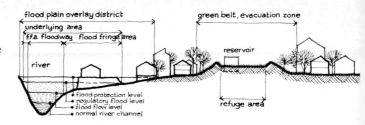

Open spaces

Which serve not only to isolate zones of potential risk from each other but also function as emergency escape and accommodation facilities, should be equally distributed throughout any large project and should, ideally, be interlinked. In areas likely to be affected by floods and storm surges, it may be necessary to include specially built refuges which can consist of built-up earth mounds large enough to protect the entire population of the project.

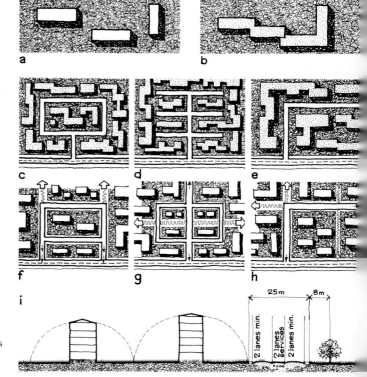

Layout must allow for free flow of elements (a is good, b is wrong) and there should never be only one exit from a building or group of buildings, no dead end streets nor built-up street corners (c–e). Better solutions are shown in f–h. Distances between buildings are important as is the provision of adequate access roads (i)

Layout In mixed development, workshops and industrial plants which constitute a risk of explosion, fire, or release of noxious materials, should not be located in, nor too close to, residential areas.

Every large development should have at least two access roads. In earthquake areas streets should be wide enough to make access of emergency vehicles (for instance fire engines) possible, even if part of the street is blocked by wreckage. Roads and footpaths in areas subject to flooding should be raised as high as possible to prevent them from being flooded. Dead end streets should be avoided.

Underpasses, overpasses, bridges and tunnels are points of potential risk and where their use is unavoidable, bypasses or alternative routes should be provided.

The layout of buildings should create the minimum obstruction to the free flow of natural elements such as flood waters and wind. The distance between buildings is important; the collapse of any structure must not endanger others, and open space should not be completely covered by possible wreckage. All buildings must be accessible to fire-fighting equipment from at least two sides and courtyards should have emergency access.

Finally, layouts should not be too complicated; they must be easily comprehended by the inhabitants (including children) to avoid confusion in times of any emergency.

Chapter 4

Technology

Site
Location

It is important to determine how accessible the site is, particularly if it is situated outside a major urban area. The means of transport to be used as well as the condition and dimensions of the access routes will largely determine the maximum size and weight of building components and, therefore, the method of construction which will be most appropriate. Check on:

● the condition of roads and bridges—they may need to be repaired or strengthened; new roads may have to be built

● the situation during the rainy season—roads may be impassable during certain periods

● the railway service, the nearest station and the road links between this and the site.

Services

In the major urban areas there will probably be no difficulty in obtaining connections to the mains supply for water, for electricity and for sewage, but on remote sites other arrangements may have to be made; the local system may be too weak or too far removed.
Check on:

● electricity—it may be necessary to generate one's own and even if there is a local supply, a standby generator may be advisable

● water—the supply, if any, may be erratic and water storage, therefore, essential. Water may have to be delivered by tanker from the nearest well or pumped from a nearby river or lake. In the latter case, conditions during the dry season in particular must be borne in mind. In both cases, water may not be potable and, therefore, require purification

● waste disposal—cesspits and soak-aways may be required

● communications—telephone and post. It can, in some places, be almost impossible to get a telephone connection or postal service to a site away from a major town.

Moroccan building, on site relatively inaccessible to brought-in materials and technologies, exploiting local resources. Walls are of battered mud construction, decorated with roughly incised brick

Drainage

Of surface waters is not given a great deal of attention in the arid areas because of the infrequency and small amount of rain.

In other tropical areas, however, it is extremely important and a storm-water system able to cope with the sudden and, often, torrential downpours must be planned. Great care must also be taken with the siting of buildings, particularly on a slope, as inadequate drainage can lead to flooding and erosion.

Soils

The soil and ground-water should be tested. Although the soils found in the hot climate areas are similar to those of the temperate zone, there are differences, particularly in the hot desert environments where absence of rain-water and high evaporation rates lead to the precipitation of salts within the soils, necessitating the use of sulphate-resisting cements and the isolation of concrete from the soil by waterproof membranes.

Expansive soils—which can usually be identified by the large cracks in the surface during the dry-season—can be a problem in dryer regions where conditions necessary for them to develop their capacity to swell occur. The clay part of these soils usually contains a mineral which absorbs water and, under certain conditions, expands considerably. The erection of a building on this soil stops evaporation and the increase in moisture content can cause the soil to swell and lift the building. The increase in moisture content is not uniform over the whole area and results in differential movement which causes distortion and serious cracking of the walls. Deep foundations, where the depth of the material is not too great, or under-reamed piles—with the structure clear of the ground in both cases—can be used. Small buildings can be either rigidly or flexibly constructed to ride out or tolerate the movement.

The following are the more important soil types most frequently encountered in hot deserts:

Gravel plains

Formed as the result of sporadic floods and consisting of unsorted gravels and cobbles, with the occasional boulder, mixed with finer material. This type of ground may not be homogeneous and can contain quite large pockets of finer grain, weaker material. In a uniform mass it has high bearing characteristics.

Inland dunes

Accumulations of wind-blown sand which can readily become cemented by the evaporation of salt bearing ground-water. Care must be taken to make sure that the cementation, which can give the soil extra strength, is consistent throughout the area of the project. In desert countries most of the urban and other development tends to take place in coastal areas where an extremely variable and often complex subsoil is found. Three main units recur over large sections of the Middle East.

● beach deposits—which can extend quite far inland. Soil varies from clean sand to material containing a large proportion of shell fragments and other organic debris. Bands of loose shells can present problems

● sabkha flats—the high water-table as well as the low density of the sand and its high salt concentration present problems, and foundations need to be protected. As the bearing properties are low, ground improvement or piling is essential

● semi-stable dunes—often uniformly cemented with good bearing properties. Although the salt content can be high, it is not as bad as in the sabkha areas.

Zones of silt and clay can be found, often 10 m or more below the surface, in all the coastal areas. Pile foundations may be required for multi-storey buildings. Rock needs to be carefully checked, as it may be merely part of the soil deposit hardened by mineral cementation.

Materials

Two basic things have to be considered when materials are selected for buildings in hot climates: availability and performance. There are obvious advantages in using local materials, not least of which are the economic ones (particularly valid in the developing lands); the avoidance of foreign exchange expenditure and the useful employment of local labour. Although the extent and rate of deterioration of building materials is caused in part by design, workmanship and use, environmental factors are a major influence and have a profound effect on the durability and behaviour of materials and structures. Materials which last well in hot, dry conditions may simply not be suitable in warm, humid areas. Moisture, temperature, ultra-violet radiation and salt-laden winds can all have a detrimental effect on materials and two or more of these elements acting together almost invariably produce greater deterioration if they were acting independently. Not only must the materials used be suitable for the specific climatic conditions involved, but the design and detailing must be appropriate to both the materials and the climatic conditions.

The grass roofs and patterned plaster walls of a group of N'debele dwellings in South Africa

Building materials in the hot climate zones

Material	Cane, leaves and grass	Timber
Availability	Cane and leaves mainly in the warm humid zones and grass in the intermediate and sub-tropical zones.	Both hardwoods and softwoods are commonly found in most tropical and sub-tropical areas with the exception of the hot dry zones where all timber and most timber products (chipboards, plywoods etc) have to be imported.
Use	Vegetable fibres of all sorts—vines, bamboo, palm fronds etc have been traditionally used for buildings in the warm humid zones and are well adapted to these climates, being waterproof, lightweight, with no heat storage, and when used for screens allow free air passage. Bamboo has been successfully used as a reinforcement in concrete.	Timber for use in buildings should always be properly seasoned and dried to approximately its equilibrium moisture content in use. Although this is necessary for all climates, failure to do so can cause exaggerated problems in hot-dry climates. On external woodwork preservative stains should be used rather than paints or varnishes which tend to deteriorate fairly rapidly in the hot zones. All woodwork should be vacuum/pressure treated, as most of the hot areas are within the termite zone. Sapwood is particularly vulnerable and should never be used unless treated.
Problems and durability	With the exception of bamboo these materials have a short lifespan, although they are relatively easy to repair and replace. Rapid deterioration due to termite attack. Fire is a problem as these materials burn easily. Thatch roofs can harbour insects and vermin.	In hot-dry zones, deterioration is usually caused by the extremes of climatic conditions. Continual dimensional changes produce checks, splits, warping and raising of the grain. Distortion of timber in these climates can be severe. Wind-blown sand and grip gradually erode exposed timber. In warm-humid zones timber is particularly susceptible to wet and dry rot and to attack by termites and beetles

Material	Metals	Asbestos cement
Availability	With some exceptions all metals required for building have to be imported in finished form. In some places door and window frames are made up from imported sections.	Locally manufactured in many of the non-temperate parts of the world.
Use	There is no excessive corrosion of most metals in hot dry climates (except in coastal zones). Aluminium and copper have good durability in all climatic regions if correctly used. The use of profiled, galvanised iron is very widespread in the tropics but is generally unsuitable for very hot climates.	Widely used as roof covering and wall cladding as well as for sun-screening components and low-pressure piping systems (particularly in soils having a high salt content).
Problems and durability	Corrosion due to high humidity in warm, wet zones and the combination of high temperatures, high humidity and salt-laden air in tropical marine areas produces severe conditions in this respect. Fatigue cracking of metals (eg lead) used in flashings and other exposed positions can be a problem.	In warm, humid regions algae tends to grow on damp sheets and leads to blackening. Sheets tend to become brittle and can be damaged by hail. High breakage rate when materials have to be transported over long distances.

Material	Glass	Plastics
Availability	Widely used and freely available but imported almost everywhere; transport costs and wastage are high.	Although many of the countries in question have abundant resources of the basic raw material—oil—plastics are, in the main, imported from the highly industrialised countries.
Use	Large areas of glass are justifiable only if adequately shaded or in regions where solar radiation is required during cold seasons.	Although plastics offer many advantages over conventional materials, the climate of the tropical zones does not favour their use externally. The insulation properties of fibreglass and some of the foamed plastics such as expanded polystyrene and polyurethane can be used to advantage. Other major potential uses are for water supply and drainage, floor coverings and electrical fittings.
Problems and durability	Wind-blown sand causes etching and abrasion in arid areas. Some of the special heat-absorbing glasses can crack if provision is not made for expansion, or if the glass is unevenly heated.	Deterioration is started by ultraviolet radiation and accelerated by high temperature. Plastics are consequently far less durable in the hot climate areas than in the temperate regions. As a result of their low resistance to abrasion, surface damage is caused by wind-blown sand. Some types are combustible and emit dangerous gases when burning.

Material	Paints	Waterproofing: bitumen and sealants
Availability	Local production of some paints in many places. Plastic based paints are usually imported.	Although bitumen is one of the by-products of oil refining, it is by no means plentiful even in the oil producing lands. The specialised waterproofing systems incorporating bituminous felt (among other things) are imported in most places.
Use	The performance of most paints is poor in hot climate regions; exposure to solar radiation and high temperatures causes them to break down more frequently than in temperate zones. Frequent repainting (particularly for roofs) is necessary and this must be kept in mind when comparing relative costs of various materials. Emulsion paints are likely to give best overall results in many instances as they allow surfaces to breathe and permit trapped moisture to escape—this can be particularly important in humid regions. Sand blasting and multicoat epoxy resin treatment is advisable for metals in humid and salt-laden atmospheres. Limewash is an excellent solar reflector and another advantage is its ability to emit long-wave radiation.	The life of these materials is much shorter than in the colder parts of the world. Built-up bituminous felt roofing systems can be badly affected by fatigue, ultra-violet degradation and water vapour build-up underneath the membranes. Advice should be obtained from manufacturers to find a system appropriate to the specific conditions. Normal mastics are not capable of retaining their elasticity in tropical conditions. The more expensive polysulphides and polyurethanes should be used for expansion joints and other applications. Bitumen is used successfully to treat timber (eg poles) and gives good protection against rot, fungi and insects.
Problems and durability	Storage in high temperatures causes separation of ingredients. Paint may fail due to incompatibility with the surface it is covering, eg it may be sufficiently flexible to withstand movement. In humid regions oil based paints (which seal the surface) may blister and peel off if moisture is trapped behind them. White paints tend to discolour (yellow) within a year or two under very hot conditions; light tints may be preferable. Dark colours absorb more heat and tend to fade. Frequent changes between rainy and sunny conditions can cause chalking. Large and frequent changes in temperature result in brittleness and cracking. Limewash is not very durable and has to be renewed regularly.	Repeated wetting and drying seriously affects visco-elasticity. Intense ultra-violet radiation can result in materials becoming brittle and eventually cracking and crumbling. Heat causes softening and blistering. Organic-based felts can decay in warm, humid conditions.

Whitewash used on a church on the island of Sifnos in the Cyclades

Material	Earth	Clay and calcium-silicate bricks
Availability	One of the most widely used traditional building materials in hot-dry lands. Some areas do not have soils containing enough clay for this purpose. Earth has been used not only for walls but also for roofs; mud brick vaults and domes are common in countries like Iran and Egypt.	Burnt clay bricks are one of the most widely used building materials throughout the tropics. Brick production is well established in many places. A number of factories producing sand-lime bricks from indigenous materials have been set up in the Gulf States.
Use	Pise and adobe are the two main construction methods used. Pise (monolithic construction): damp earth is laid between formwork and compacted by ramming. High sand content, density and low moisture content after ramming reduces problem of cracking. Walls need to be thicker than for adobe. Adobe: sun dried mud bricks which are allowed to shrink before being laid in the wall; soil with a high clay content is required.	Considerable differences in size, shape, material composition and quality. Calcium-silicate bricks are more expensive than concrete blocks but can be used as external facings without rendering and are more durable. Not used for load-bearing walls in buildings over one storey. Textured and pigmented bricks are available.
Problems and durability	Surface cracking of adobe walls. High risk of termite damage in some areas which can be reduced by addition of a small amount of cement. Walls exposed to weathering and rain require frequent repair work. Some water-proofing can be obtained by using cement or lime renderings. Earth can be stabilised by using small quantities of cement or bitumen.	Particularly in warm, humid climates some bricks may be suitable only for internal use. Clay bricks can be penetrated by continuous driving rain.

93

Concrete in various forms
used in an African
seminary

Material	Concrete blocks	Concrete
Availability	The scarcity of natural clay deposits in many places (eg much of the Middle East) has led to the widespread use of locally manufactured concrete blocks.	Concrete and reinforced concrete are widely used throughout the non-temperate zones. Cement is manufactured locally in many places and imported at a very high cost in others. Sand is found almost everywhere but may be contaminated with soluble salts. Gravel is difficult to come by in some areas and problems can arise with transportation which may be erratic and unreliable. The large amounts of water needed can present the greatest difficulties in hot arid areas where much of the available water is either salty or brackish and considered unsuitable for concrete work.
Use	Both solid and hollow blocks are available. Quality tends to be low but blocks are generally not used for load-bearing walls. Some contractors prefer to manufacture blocks on site to keep maximum control on quality.	In hot climates concrete can deteriorate rapidly as a result of minerals, water, bad workmanship and climate. High temperatures accelerate chemical reactions, large diurnal temperature differences cause considerable movements, hot winds can dry the concrete too rapidly and high humidities can saturate it. Expert advice should be sought. The use of sulphate resisting cement may be required. Water and aggregates must be closely controlled. Sample testing must be constantly undertaken.
Problems and durability	Cracking due to shrinkage caused by temperature fluctuations.	In areas of high humidity concrete may set prematurely in the concrete

Shiny metal roofs are usually good reflectors only while new and a galvanised iron roof like the one shown may need to be painted some light colour at regular intervals

Surfaces exposed to driving rain have limited impermeability and should be rendered.

sacks. Considerable movement can lead to pronounced cracking either in the concrete itself or in adjacent parts of the structure.

Salts in aggregate and water can cause corrosion of the reinforcement and subsequent spalling of the concrete cover.

In hot dry areas the rapid evaporation and shortage of water makes proper curing difficult and can result in low strength, cracking and high permeability.

Damage to concrete near or below ground due to salts or humic acids (in hot, humid areas) present in the soil.

Material	Plaster	Stone
Availability	Used everywhere (see also concrete).	A wide variety of building stone is found throughout the tropics with the exception of the low-lands in warm, humid zones and some sandy parts of the arid zones.
Use	Sand-cement plaster most commonly used. Lack of skilled plasterers in many places makes the use of lime and gypsum difficult because of their fast set in high temperatures.	Used mainly as decorative facing and for landscape work as although the material is often cheap, labour costs can be very high.
Problems and durability	Sand-cement plasters are brittle and have a high drying shrinkage rate accelerated by improper curing— they are, therefore, vulnerable to cracking. Difference in rate of heating and cooling between rendering and backing loosens bond, results in spalling.	Can be difficult to find good stone-masons. High temperatures may sometimes cause cracking.

Various aspects have already been discussed under climate. Some additional requirements are noted here.

Frame The use of structural steel tends to be confined to industrial buildings with the most common structural system for large buildings being a reinforced concrete framework.
● Formwork is most often of timber boarding erected by carpenters and any special or sophisticated shuttering would probably have to be imported.
● Provision should be made for the structural movement which is caused by the intense solar radiation and large diurnal variations. In the hot-dry zones there can be a marked drop in temperature within a few hours once the sun sets, while in the humid areas temperature can be reduced very quickly by a heavy downpour. The stresses resulting from these continued rapid changes can cause bad cracks to develop; sliding joints (for instance between brick load-bearing walls and concrete slabs) and expansion joints, in reinforced concrete structures, must be carefully planned and detailed. Fibrous material together with suitable sealants can be used to fill expansion joints.
● Where there is danger of concrete being damaged by soluble salts—sulphates and chlorides—in the soil, it should be protected below ground level by a suitable bituminous emulsion.

Walls In hot-dry areas where heavy walls are called for, various types of clay, stone and brick have been traditionally used but have, in many places, been replaced by concrete or concrete blocks. Although cavity wall construction can be effective if properly designed, the simplest solution for these zones is to follow tradition and to use the thickest suitable walls.

Givoni suggests that the most satisfactory solution may be composite walls consisting of a heavyweight internal layer externally insulated by rockwool or expanded plastic, which is protected by an outer waterproof skin. This type of construction would restrict the rate of heat flow and reduce the amount of heat absorbed by the inner wall during the daytime. It would, however, also restrict the heat flow in the reverse direction at night and particularly good ventilation would be needed to ensure that buildings of this construction do not become much warmer at night than those with a simple solid wall.

96

In hot, humid areas modern lightweight frame construction clad with thin panels are most often used; the cavity may be a problem, as it can harbour insects and vermin.

Roof Because of its orientation, comparatively large area and the difficulty of shading it from the intense solar radiation, the roof is often a major source of heat gain in a building. It should, therefore, absorb as little radiant heat as possible and offer good resistance to heat flow from outside to inside.

●Whatever the type of roof, the use of a reflective upper surface is important. Asbestos cement sheets and galvanised iron provide reasonable reflection only when new and will need to be painted white or some other light colour at regular intervals. On a pitched roof, light-coloured paints and shiny metals (eg aluminium) can create a glare problem in the vicinity.

●In lightweight roof constructions, thermal insulation with a reflective upper surface (eg aluminium foil) at ceiling level is without doubt the most effective way of reducing room temperatures. In areas where dust is a problem, however, the reflectivity of the foil can be rapidly reduced as dust collects on its upper surfaces. To overcome this problem, the foil can be suspended above the ceiling so that both of its surfaces face air spaces; in this way not only are two air spaces created, but the heat emission from the shiny underside of the foil will remain low. The simplest procedure is to drape the foil over the ceiling brandering or the structural members of the roof. Fibreglass matting, or some other suitable insulation material, should be laid on top of the ceiling boards.

●As heat is transferred downward from the roof covering mainly by radiation and as convection plays a minor role, many researchers feel that natural ventilation of the roof space does not have much value. This does not mean, however, that ventilation of the roof space is unnecessary; it is, in fact, essential under certain climatic conditions to minimise the possibility of condensation on the inside of the roof covering. Roofing materials such as galvanised steel (and even asbestos cement) can easily cool down to below outdoor air temperatures on clear nights as a result of heat radiation to the sky and this inevitably increases the possibility of condensation occurring.

●A problem of corrugated sheet metal roofs—particularly those with a long span—can be the noise generated during a heavy rainstorm. This nuisance can be reduced by shortening the spans and coating the underside of the sheets with bitumen to reduce reverberation.

Harold Hay's Skytherm system which consists of water filled polythene bags on a steel ribbed roofing, covered with 50 mm thick polyurethane panels which slide on tracks (**a**). Winter heating (**b** and **c**) and summer protection (**d** and **e**)

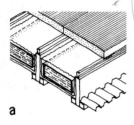

a

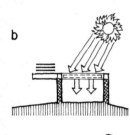

b

c

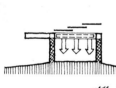

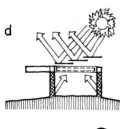

d

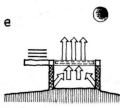

e

●In areas subject to heavy rainfalls, gutters can be a problem and are prohibited or discouraged in some places. With wide roof overhangs, water can be freely shed from the roof on to paved surfaces. Valley gutters should have adequate falls.

●Massive and heavyweight roofs are generally flat and of reinforced concrete. Various methods are used to reduce heat flow and to increase the time-lag, and some form of insulation applied to the outside of the slab not only reduces heat gains through the roof but also thermal movement of the roof itself. A layer of earth covering the slab is one method commonly used in the Middle East. In his book, *Architecture in Tropical Australia*, Saini suggests that grass or some other form of vegetation grown on the roof cools the air above the roof and the roots preserve a certain amount of moisture, which both helps to keep the temperature down and prolongs the life of the concrete by minimising cracking in periods of extreme temperature variation.

●Permanent pools of water and rotating type water sprays have also been used to modify the thermal performance of roofs, but the cost involved and the shortage of water in hot, dry climates are the main disadvantages of these solutions. A system patented by Harold Hay (the *Skytherm Roof Pond*) consists of water-filled polythene bags placed on the roof and a movable covering of 50 mm thick polyurethane insulating panels. In winter, these panels are left open during the day to allow solar radiation to be absorbed and re-radiated into the building; at night the panels are closed to conserve the heat. In summer the process is reversed with the panels being closed during the day to insulate the bags from solar radiation and allow heat to be drawn from inside, while at night they are left open to allow the water to radiate heat to the night sky.

●Lightweight concrete is widely used for providing insulating roof screeds. In places such as the Gulf States, where there are no naturally occurring lightweight aggregates, gas entrainment has to be used either by incorporating aluminium powder into the mix or by introducing a chemical foam, which is the best method for in situ work. The usual difficulties associated with hot weather curing are aggravated with aerated concrete.

●As the flat roof is frequently used for outdoor living, suitable trafficable surface finish should be provided. The light coloured concrete tiles, often used for this purpose, also provide protection from solar radiation for waterproofing membranes.

●Shading devices are sometimes used to reduce the absorption of solar radiation at the roof surface. These devices can be light or heavy; they can be fixed, adjustable or retractable; exclude from view by parapet walls or project over the roof edge to provide shading for walls and openings. One cheap and practical system which has been tested consists of a series of reed panels on bamboo frames. Although the panels require regular maintenance they were found to provide a significant improvement.

● The temperature of the layer of air above a flat roof may drop below the air temperature at night and can be utilised to cool the building by allowing the roof to slope downward toward the internal courtyard. In this way the cool air is channelled into the rooms via the courtyard. To keep warmer external air from flowing in, the roof can be surrounded by a parapet wall at its upper edge.

● Sand can block rain-water outlets on flat roofs. Adequately dimensioned spouts or gargoyles are the simplest way of shedding water from the roof, but they should project far enough beyond the building to avoid water splashing on to walls.

Underground buildings

In the hot-arid zones there is a revival of interest in the principle of building structures underground—a system that has been used for thousands of years. In parts of Tunisia, for example, is an area of crater-like pits which resemble a lunar landscape; these are the entrances and central courtyards of the dwellings of the Matmata, who have lived like this for at least 2000 years. These people, according to the Life book *The Deserts*,

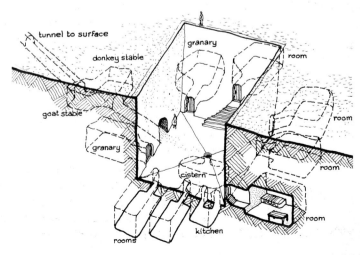

Diagrammatic illustration of a typical Matmata dwelling with various rooms carved out of the earth around a 10–15 m square, sunken courtyard

Plan, section and diagrammatic perspective of Malcolm Wells' underground office completed in 1973

(Below) Wells maintains that earth should not be retained by big parapets as, aside of anything else, a great deal of heat can be gained or lost through the structure (**a**). Although the approach in **b** is better, the best solution is smaller windows, louvred sunshades, and a properly insulated structure (**c**)

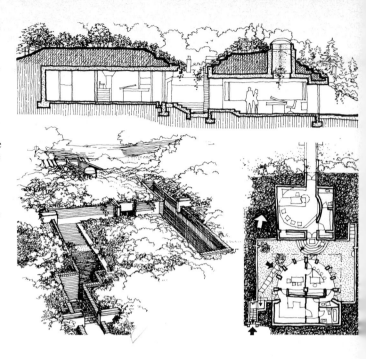

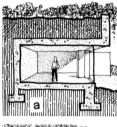

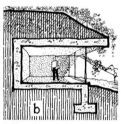

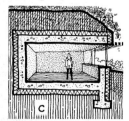

stubbornly resist all attempts to move them from these dwellings which are so well insulated against the scorching desert days and chilly nights.

Over the past 40 years whole towns and villages—including not only dwellings but also factories, schools, hotels and offices— have been built entirely underground in the loess (silt) bed of northern China. In America contemporary versions range from Soleri's *Dome house* (1949), which is partly sunken into the Arizona desert, and his *Earth house*, which is part of the Cosanti Foundation in Scottsdale, to a variety of more truly underground buildings designed by Malcolm Wells and other architects who specialise in this type of structure. In South Australia at Coober Pedy almost half the houses of the copal miners are underground, carved into the soft clay stone of the area.

Underground structures make use of earth covered walls and roofs to protect the interior from radiation and provide a huge thermal mass to stabilise air temperatures. At a depth of about 2·5 m below ground level, the temperature of the earth is remarkably even and remains close to the average yearly temperature of the region, so providing relative warmth in

100

winter and coolness in summer. Soil temperatures are not only moderate at this depth, but they also change very slowly with the maximum and minimum temperatures occurring up to three months later than those on the surface.

Although building an underground house is not particularly complicated, it does have its own peculiar problems: weight, when for instance roofs have to carry up to 2 m of earth, as well as the problems of waterproofing, cross ventilation (wind catchers, ventilation ducts, evaporative coolers and sunken courtyards would seem to be the solution) and insulation. The roof and the tops of walls need to be insulated to protect the interior from the faster temperature swings near the surface, while the lower parts of walls and the floor can be more exposed to the much slower temperature variations that take place deeper down.

Solar energy

Solar energy can contribute greatly to an improvement in living conditions in the developing countries, all the more so because these countries are generally blessed with an abundance of sunshine. Not only do many of the countries in question have summer rainfall, but during winter the sky is usually cloud-free and radiation is thus available when it is most required. The use of solar energy for local applications (eg water heating and distillation) by means of small units is by far the most realistic approach, particularly in the developing countries.

Water heating

Heating system:

All solar water heaters consist basically of the solar collector which absorbs solar radiation during the day and transfers heat to the water, and a well-insulated tank where the water can be stored with little temperature loss until it is required. Various types of absorber units are found, but the relatively simple flat-plate collector is most commonly used. The proportion of diffused radiation is high in many places—often more than 25 per cent of the annual total—and it is therefore important that collectors be capable of utilising diffuse as well as direct radiation. In this respect flat-plate collectors are very suitable.

The collector normally consists of the following components:

● The absorber or heat-exchanger element: usually a sheet of more or less flat material constructed in such a way that channels are formed through which the water can circulate. The exposed surface should absorb the maximum amount of radiation, but should not easily re-radiate. Electro-chemical treatment is best, but as it is expensive a matt black acrylic emulsion paint is often used.

● Insulation: heat losses to the rear are normally minimised by placing a layer of insulation behind the unexposed side of the collector plate.

● Transparent cover: to reduce convection and low-temperature radiation heat losses from the absorber surface, it is necessary to cover it with a sheet of glass or suitable plastic.

● Absorber box: or weatherproof container to prevent rain from affecting the insulation and to provide a support for the transparent cover.

Design procedures and installation:

● Calculate the daily requirement for hot water. If electric boosting is provided, storage should approximately equal the daily requirement. With unboosted heating, storage for an additional 20 per cent is advisable.

● Choose the type of collector to be used and calculate the number of panels that will be required; the intensity of solar radiation available and the efficiency of the chosen collectors will affect this calculation. Generally it can be estimated that 1 m² of absorbed area will produce between 50–75 l of water at roughly 50–60°C per day.

● Collectors must always face as close to true North or South (in the southern and northern hemispheres respectively) as possible. Significant efficiency losses will occur if the units face more than 10° off this orientation.

● Collectors should be inclined to the horizontal, usually by an angle equal to the latitude plus 10°. This angle is chosen mainly to facilitate the collection of solar heat during the winter when the sun is fairly low in the sky.

● The ideal position will be protected from wind and free of shadows cast by trees and buildings. The collectors should also be as close as possible to the storage tank and to the areas where the hot water is required in the building.

● The circulation of the water is maintained by the so-called thermosiphon effect which largely depends on the temperature differences between the water in the collectors and the water in the storage tank and the height of the storage tank above the absorber. As the pressure is fairly small, any obstruction or accumulation of air bubbles in the system will usually impede the natural flow.

102

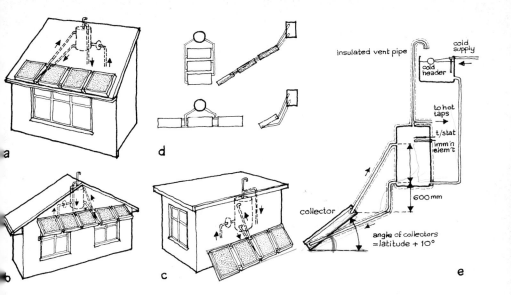

a

b

c

d

insulated vent pipe

cold
supply

cold
header

to hot
taps

t/stat

imm'n
elem't

600 mm

collector

angle of collectors
= latitude + 10°

e

Collectors can be mounted on the roof or as awnings with the storage tank in the roof space in both cases (**a** and **b**) or on the ground with the tank built into a cupboard (**c**). Two possible methods of connecting a series of collectors (**d**) and a schematic layout of a solar water heating system (**e**)

Below) Solar collectors must be located outside the shadow areas of surrounding trees

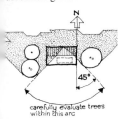

carefully evaluate trees within this arc

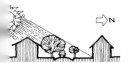

It is important to ensure that:

● there is a continuous rise (at least 20 mm per metre) in both the flow and return pipes from the collectors to the tank. The horizontal channels or pipes in the collector itself must also slope upwards

● the bottom of the tank should be at least 0·6 m above the top of the collectors; this helps to minimise reverse flow at night which can cool the hot water in the tank

● where the collectors have to be mounted above the hot water tank a small pump will be needed to circulate the water

● Pitched roof: collectors can be placed flat on the roof close to the eaves to allow space for installation of the storage tank above them and within the roof space.

● Flat roof: to provide the collectors with the required tilt and the tank(s) with the necessary elevation, both must be mounted on supporting structures.

● Wall mounting: collectors can be used to provide shade for openings. If hinged and provided with flexible pipe connectors, the angle of tilt can be adjusted at regular intervals (approximately every 2 months) so that the collector face is almost always at right angles to the sun at its highest.

● If it is feasible to do so without using long pipe lines, collectors can be situated at ground level.

103

● The storage tank must be placed as close to the collector as possible and both pipes should follow the most direct route that is convenient, avoiding sharp bends. The total length of pipes should not exceed 15 m. To ensure an adequate flow all pipes should be generously sized and the following is intended as a general guide:

For storage capacity up to

150 1—bore 25 mm
150–200 1—bore 32 mm
250–500 1—bore 40 mm

● Circulation pipes and storage tanks should be well insulated to reduce heat loss.
● Tanks should have the following connections:
  ● cold water supply at bottom—positioned so that water discharges horizontally or slightly downward. A diffusing device or baffle attached to the outlet within the tank reduces turbulence and the mixing of the incoming cold water and the hot water in the tank
  ● vent pipe, to which hot water supply is attached, at top: should be at least 20 mm in diameter and should be provided with 180° bend
  ● return pipe to absorber at lowest point of tank
  ● flow pipe from absorber two-thirds of the way up the tank
  ● electric immersion element and thermostat for auxiliary heating on dull days. In solar storage tanks these should be mounted two-thirds to three-quarters of the way up the tank—preferably slightly above the flow pipe inlet from the collector.
● The long axis of the tank should not be mounted horizontally except as a last resort.
● Although the mass of each collector unit filled with water is not very large, the load should be evenly distributed on a roof particularly if there is a large number of collectors in the system
● In hail belts glass-covered collectors should be protected by a 13 mm wire mesh screen suspended in a framework at least 30 mm above the glass. This form of screen reduces the effective absorber area by approximately 15% and compensation will have to be made for this. Wire-reinforced glass must not be used since it does not transmit solar radiation satisfactorily.

Solar stills

Apart from solar water heating, the main application for solar energy in the non-temperate zones would seem to be for the distillation of brackish or sea water.

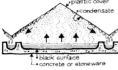

plastic cover
condensate
black surface
concrete or stoneware

Section through a typical
solar still

The conventional still consists of a shallow container—or a series of shallow trays—which a black surface covered with a transparent sloping roof of glass or plastic. Water places in the container is heated and evaporates. The vapour rises and condenses on the underside of the transparent cover along which it runs into channels or gutters at the edges. Units of this type can deliver about 5 l per day per m² under hot conditions and, since they are cheap and simple, have obvious advantages, particularly in the hot, arid lands.

Water distillation has been used in the experimental *Ecol house* built by the Minimum Cost Housing Group (School of Architecture, McGill University)—the roof over the bathroom unit is a combination rainwater collector and solar still. Rainwater runs from the roof into a storage drum, is used for showering, after which it is collected in a holding tank. This dirty water is then pumped by hand to the still and, after being distilled, the pure water is used for drinking, cooking and dish washing.

Water

The earth is uniquely endowed with large quantities of water in its liquid state: over 1·3 billion cubic kilometres, in fact, which cycles and recycles continuously. It evaporates from the sea and land, is drawn into the atmosphere, falls as rain and snow, sinks into the earth to reappear in watercourses, and then drains back to the sea; it is used, disposed of, purified and used again. Men cannot 'use up' water and the total supply neither grows nor diminishes. Two things are of concern, however: the uneven distribution of water and what gets dissolved or suspended in it.

The quality of fresh water available in any country depends on the annual precipitation or, in other words, the amount of rain which falls on the land. Although the amount of rain that many parts of the world receive is a great deal more than net consumption and might seem adequate for the time being, between 50 and 70 per cent is lost through evaporation and transpiration by plants. Possible water, therefore, is not actual water and the problem is made worse through uneven distribution and poor catchments, while much of what is captured becomes useless through pollution.

As a result of these problems, and in spite of the large amounts of water potentially available, water scarcities have plagued man throughout history and afflict him even more today. This is

(Right) Underground concrete cistern for rainwater with slow sand filter which includes a pyramid galvanised screen—this distributes the water evenly over the sand bed. Above the sand filter is a small tank to receive the first run off

particularly true of the hot areas of the world: in the arid zones rain may not fall for years and general, widespread or gentle falls are almost unknown. When it does come, precipitation is usually in the form of violent downpours, seldom lasting much more than an hour, and the hard-baked ground cannot absorb the water. Water in these areas often has to be piped over very long distances or else obtained from wells or boreholes.

The problem in the humid zones is usually one of contamination: water here is usually obtained from streams, rivers and lakes which are often foul and a breeding ground for diseases. It is important, therefore, for the designer to consider ways of not only collecting and storing rainwater but also conserving water through various means.

Collection, storage and purification

Collection   Roofs that are going to be used as catchment areas must be constructed of satisfactory materials—for example corrugated galvanised steel or asbestos cement—and well maintained in order to minimise the risk of contamination. Gutters and downpipes must be protected against corrosion and lead must not be used for any part of the system.

Storage   Once the effective (horizontal) area of the roof and the average monthly rainfall are known, then it is possible to calculate the quantities of water which can be collected and decide on the size of a storage tank. Where water is also collected from paved surfaces (eg a courtyard) it may be necessary to keep this stored separately from roof water.

Storage tanks or cisterns can be prefabricated of either galvanised steel or asbestos cement or built of brick or concrete, and may be placed in the roof space, at ground level or underground. Underground cisterns have the advantage of keeping the stored water cool and sweet.

The tanks or cisterns should be covered and well sealed to ensure, among other things, that mosquitoes cannot breed in them. A small vent, covered by fine copper insect mesh, should be provided to allow air displaced by the water to escape, and the floor of the tank should be sloped towards an outlet at the bottom to facilitate cleaning. Water should, ideally, pass through a fine wire mesh screen and a settling chamber to

106

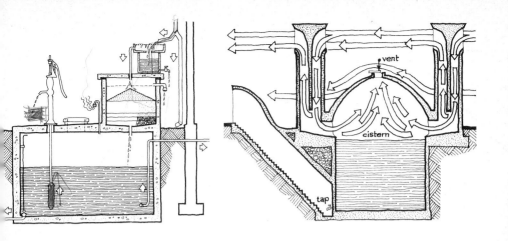

prevent bird droppings and other organic material from entering the storage tank.

Use   If the approximate consumption per person per day for all purposes is ascertained and the amount that can be collected has been calculated, it will be possible to decide what the rain-water is to be used for. Untreated it can be used for the garden, toilet flushing or washing—provided it cannot accidentally be used for drinking purposes—but if it is to be used for drinking and cooking, it will have to be purified.

Purification   Is required not only to remove suspended solids and impurities which may affect the taste, but also to remove bacteria. One method of purifying the water is by distillation, as described in the previous section of this chapter. The alternative is filtration—usually through a slow sand filter which removes the majority of suspended solids and bacteria—and some sterilis-ation or tertiary treatment.

Above right) Underground istern in Iran covered by a domed roof and surrounded by a number of wind towers. In summer draughts ensure continuous evaporation from the water surface and the lower layers of water are kept cool

The simplest method of sterilisation is to boil the water, but this leaves it flat and tasteless. Another method, which tends to be rather complicated for domestic use, is chlorination. The most practical solution is to use a ready-made filter candle—a hollow ceramic cylinder impregnated with activated silver—which can be attached to a tap or sink fitting and is very effective, producing high purity water.

Conservation   There are various ways in which water can be conserved and only a brief description of some of these are given here.

(Right) Diagrammatic section through the Clivus Multrum composting toilet. Made of fibreglass in two parts with an optional midsection, it requires a little over 2 m headroom

(Right below) A great deal of water can be saved by installing showers rather than baths

(Far right) A diagrammatic illustration of the water collection, distillation and recycling method used in the experimental Ecol house (see text)

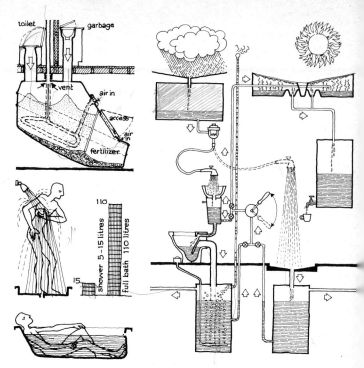

Toilet flushing	Almost a third of domestic water usage is for this purpose and great savings could be made if the cistern capacity were reduced or if one of the various methods of waste disposal was considered. Toilet flushing is a waste of purified water and it is an ideal way of re-using water already used for showering and hand-washing, for instance.
Showers	Should, wherever possible, be installed in preference to baths, as they use less water.
Atomisation	Atomising sprays—in which air pressure breaks up the water into a fine spray—or spray taps can be utilised for hand washing.
Re-use and recycling	Ways in which this can be done have already been described. A good example of a simple and economical system is that demonstrated in the experimental Ecol house.

Labour

The availability, quality, quantity and efficiency of the labour to a large extent determine the mode of the building. They also affect the standards of finish and the cost of building.

● The quality of construction in many of the developing areas is poor.

● Many of the materials and components used are sub-standard.

● There are not the skilled craftsman available to install sophisticated or unusual components and equipment.

● In remote locations labour may be difficult to find and in this situation it may not be possible to compensate for the shortage of manual labour by increased use of machinery.

● Sophisticated technological equipment requires sophisticated maintenance and spares, neither of which may be available.

Building regulations and standards

There are as yet no building regulations or standards in most parts of the developing world and although it is compulsory, virtually everywhere, to submit building plans to municipal authorities for approval, examination may be confined to town planning matters. Various codes and standards may be acceptable—it is often usual for buildings to be designed and constructed in accordance with those prevailing in the home country of the consultants—and it is advisable for the architect to clarify the situation as early as possible. Specifiers must remember, however, that a building product, component or method which has been approved as being suitable for use in a temperate region may not be suitable for the environmental conditions that exist in non-temperate areas.

● All specifications should conform to local standards where they exist. Specification generally follows British, German or American practice, and it is these codes that are likely to be the basis of local regulations in the future.

● Particular care must be paid to the design, mixing and placing of concrete (also blockwork, screeds, rendering etc) as it is for the consultant to ensure that proper controls are implemented.

● Long delays in construction can be caused if products are specified which may be subject to manufacturing hold-ups and for which it may be difficult to get replacements for items broken during shipping or handling on site.

● Wherever possible simple components that are easy to install and are reasonably maintenance free should be specified.

● When complex equipment is used it is important to ensure that the supplier provides operating and maintenance instructions in the local language.

● Knowledge and awareness of local 'cottage' industries is advantageous.

Heat transfer—some basic calculations

Thermal conductivity (k-value)

This property of a material indicates the amount of heat passing through 1 m thickness of 1 m² of the material, per unit time, given a difference of 1°C in the temperature of the two opposite faces. This can be expressed in terms of $Jm/m^2/sec/°C$ (or $J/m\ sec°C$), but since the power unit Watt incorporates a time unit in its denominator (w = J/sec) the expression is simplified to W/m°C. The value varies from 0·03 W/m°C for an insulating material such as mineral wool to 53 W/m°C (or more) for steel.

Thermal resistivity

This property of a material is the reciprocal of its conductivity and indicates the time required for the transmission of one unit of heat through the same piece of material, given a difference of 1°C in the temperature of the two opposite faces. Therefore resistivity equals $\frac{1}{k}$ and is expressed in units of m°C/W.

Thermal transmittance (U-value)

This indicates the total amount of heat transmitted from air to air through a given wall or roof construction per m² surface area per time unit. U-value is influenced by not only the thermal resistance (the product of the thickness and resistivity: $R = dx\frac{1}{k} = \frac{d}{k}$) of the component parts of the construction, but also by their ability to absorb and emit heat through the external and internal surfaces (the thermal resistances of these surfaces). Put simply, the overall thermal transmittance of a homogenous material *in shade* is calculated as follows:

$$U = \frac{1}{\text{(Resistance of first surface)} + \text{(Resistivity thickness)} + \text{(Resistance of second surface)}}$$

and is expressed in terms of W/m²°C. It provides a useful unit for comparing the insulation values of various building elements (the lower the U-value, the higher the insulating value) and establishing criteria for minimum standards. In the case of more complex components, the thermal resistances of individual layers and air spaces that may be contained within the component are included in the U-value which may be calculated from the following equation:

$$U = \frac{1}{\frac{1}{h_i} + \left(\frac{1}{C_1} + \frac{1}{C_2} + \cdots \frac{1}{C_n}\right) + \left(\frac{d_1}{k_1} + \frac{d_2}{k_2} + \cdots \frac{d_n}{k_n}\right) + \frac{1}{h_o}}\ W/m^2°C$$

h = coefficient of heat transfer for the inner surface of the wall, roof or floor in W/m²°C.
$C_1, C_2 \ldots C_n$ = thermal conductances of n separate air spaces in the structure in W/m²°C (for solid components these terms fall away).
$k_1, k_2 \ldots k_n$ = thermal conductivities of n successive layers of different materials comprising the component, in W/m°C.
$d_1, d_2 \ldots d_n$ = thicknesses of n successive layers of different materials comprising the component, in metres.
h_o = coefficient of heat transfer for the outer surface of the wall, roof or floor in W/m²°C (for internal walls $h_i = h_o$).

The surface coefficients, thermal conductances of air spaces and thermal conductivities of the more common building materials are given in various sources including The *AJ Metric Handbook* published by The Architectural Press.

Radiation

The radiant heat transfer is influenced by the absorptivity (denoted by a), reflectivity (denoted by r) and emissivity (denoted by e) of the receiving surface of any opaque material. Most surfaces absorb only part of the radiation and they receive and reflect the remainder. The sum of a and r is always one ($a + r = 1$). For a theoretically perfect reflector—which would be light coloured, smooth and shiny—$r = 1$ and $a = 0$, while for the theoretically perfect absorber (or perfectly black surface) $r = 0$ and $a = 1$.

Emissivity (e) expresses the relative power of the material to emit radiant energy. For any specific wavelength of radiation its value is the same as for absorbence (ie $a = e$) but both may vary for different wavelengths. The wavelength of radiation depends on the temperature of the body emitting it and while solar radiation is short-wave, that emitted by surfaces at normal temperatures is long-wave. This means that the absorbence for solar radiation will not be the same as the emittance at normal temperatures. For example:

Surface	a or e		r
	low-temp radiation	solar radiation	solar radiation
Bright aluminium	0·05	0·20	0·80
White paint	0·09	0·30	0·70

This means that although the aluminium and white painted surfaces will each absorb and reflect similar mounts of solar radiation, the latter will emit more of the absorbed heat, which explains why it is a superior material for use on external surfaces. The low absorptivity and emissivity of bright aluminium for long-wave radiation, however, makes it an ideal material for insulation in roofs and cavity walls as long as one side faces an air space and remains clean.

Sol-air temperature

Heat transfer into the outer surface of building elements exposed to solar radiation will obviously be higher than that into similar shaded elements. For building design purposes the heating effect of radiation incident on the building should be combined with that of the outdoor air. For this purpose the sol-air temperature concept is used. The simplified formula is as follows:

$$t_{sa} = t_o + \frac{I \times a}{h_o}$$

t_{sa} = sol-air temperature in °C.
t_o = outside air temperature in °C.
I = radiation intensity on the surface in W/m²
a = absorbence of the surface
h_o = surface coefficient in W/m²°C.

Heat gain or loss

In tropical climates concern with heat gain in buildings will dominate except during cold periods (evenings, in some places, and winter months) where heat loss can be a problem. The total heat gain or loss can be calculated as follows:

$$Q_i + Q_s \pm Q_c \pm Q_v \pm Q_m - Q_e = 0 = \text{Thermal balance.}$$

If the sum of the equation is either more or less than zero then the building will obviously be either heating up or cooling.

Q_i = internal heat gain or heat output of internal sources (human bodies, lights, etc) in Watt.

Q_s = solar heat gain through windows. If the intensity of solar radiation (I) incident on the windows is known the heat gain can be calculated as follows:

The heat exchange between a building and the environment

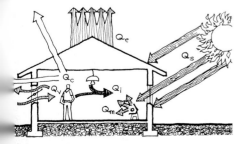

$Q_s = I \times A \times \theta$
A = area of window in m²
I = intensity of solar radiation in W/m²
θ = solar gain factor of the glass which depends on the type of glass and the angle of incidence.

Q_c = the heat flow rate in Watt, either inwards or outwards, through roof, walls or floor. This can be calculated for each element with the following equation:

$Q_c = A \times U \times \Delta t$
A = surface area of element in m²
U = transmittance value in W/m²°C
Δt = air temperature difference ($t_o - t_i$ for heat gain). If the effects of solar radiation are included and the sol-air temperature concept is used then $t_{sa} - t_i$. (Not applicable to translucent materials.)

Q_v = the convective heat flow rate in Watt due to ventilation, which can be calculated as follows:

$Q_v = 1300 \times V \times \Delta t$
1300 = volumetric specific heat of air in J/m³°C.
V = ventilation rate in m³/s (the product of the number of changes per hour—divided by 3600—and the volume of the space).
Δt = air temperature difference in °C.

Q_m = the heat flow rate in Watt of any mechanical heating or cooling equipment.

Q_e = the rate of cooling by evaporation from, for example, a roof pond, fountain or human perspiration. As it is dependent on many variables and therefore difficult to calculate, it is most often omitted or only qualitatively applied.

Steady state conditions

All the above is only valid if both indoor and outdoor temperatures remain constant and are based on an assumption of steady state conditions. This is obviously seldom the case, as the outdoor climate never remains constant over long periods. The calculation can, however, be applied in certain instances:

1 when the indoor temperature is kept constant by air conditioning in a warm-humid climate or by heating during winter in a cold climate;

2 when the building elements have a small heat-storing capacity in comparison with the total heat flow (eg light structures);

3 to determine, under normal conditions, the maximum rate of heat loss or gain and as preliminary study leading to an understanding of the more complex heat transfer problems under periodically fluctuating conditions.

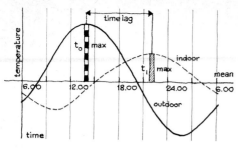

Time lag and decrement
factor

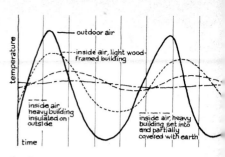

Outdoor temperature
fluctuation and its effect
on the indoor
temperature for various
types of construction

Heat storing capacity

Under conditions of daily fluctuation in temperature
and solar radiation intensity, U-value is not by itself
an accurate indication of the thermal performance of
an element, as its heat-storing capacity also plays an
important role. As a result of the approximately
repetitive 24-hour cycle of increasing and decreasing
outdoor temperature, there is a daily pattern of heat
flow into and out of any building, and there is a
marked difference between the thermal performances
of heavy and light structures under these conditions.

It takes time for the heat gained at the outside surface
to be transferred to any emitted from the inside
surface; there is in other words a time-lag which
will be small for light structures and thin elements and
larger for a massive structure.

It is also important to note that the daily variations in
temperature and rate of heat flow at the inner surface
of the building element are smaller in magnitude than
those at its outer surface and that they fall off
exponentially as the waves travel through the material. The rate at which this takes place is determined
by the decrement factor.

$$\text{Decrement factor} = \frac{t_i\ max}{t_o\ max} \qquad \text{(taken from the daily mean)}$$

As has already been explained in Chapter 2, the
designer should attempt to avoid heat gain through
the structure during overheated periods, but allow it
when there are heat losses through other channels
such as, for example, ventilation. It is, therefore,
important to select a construction with an appropriate
time-lag.

The calculations for time-lag, decrement factor and
periodic heat flow are rather involved and are
not included here. They can be found in various
sources including *The Manual of Tropical Housing* by
Koenigsberger *et al* (see Bibliography), as can values
for time-lag and the decrement factor for various
forms of construction.

Appendix 2
Building research centres

The following list includes only the principal centres dealing with the problems of building in hot climates.

International organisations

Centre for Housing, Building and Planning, United Nations, New York 10017, NY, USA

International Council for Building Research, Studies and Documentation (CIB), Weena 704, Post Office Box 20704, Rotterdam, Netherlands

International Union of Testing and Research, Laboratories for Materials and Structures (RILEM), 12 Rue Brancion, Paris 15e, France

United Nations: Office of the Disaster Relief Coordinator (UNDRO), Palais des Nations, CH-1211 Geneva 10, Switzerland

United Nations: Office of Technical Co-operation (OTC)

United Nations, New York 10017, NY, USA

Argentina Department of Research and Technology of the State Secretariat for Housing, Ministerio de Bienestar Social, Buenos Aires

Australia Commonwealth Scientific and Industrial Research Organisation, Division of Building Research, Post Office Box 56, Melbourne, Victoria 3190

Brazil Institute for Technological Research, Caixa Postal 7141, 05508 São Paulo

Egypt Centre for Housing, Building and Planning Research, Tahrir Street, Dokky, Giza

England Building Research Establishment (BRE), Garston, Watford WD2 7JR

Ethiopia Ethio-Swedish Institute of Building Technology, Post Office Box 518, Addis Ababa

Ghana CSIR Building and Road Research Institute, University Post Box 40, UST, Kumasi

India Council of Scientific and Industrial Research, Central Building Research Institute (CBRI), Roorkee UP)

Indonesia National Building Research Institute, 124 Jalan Tamansari, Bandung

Iran Institute of Standards and Industrial Research of Iran, Post Office Box 2937, Teheran

Ministry of Housing and Urban Development, Building and Housing Research Centre, Post Office Box 15-1114, Teheran

Iraq Building Research Centre: Scientific Research Foundation, Post Office Box 127, Al Jadriha, Baghdad

Israel Building Research Station TECHNION, Israel Institute of Technology, Technion City, Haifa

Building and Techniques Research Institute, 200 Dizengoff Road, Post Office Box 3082, Tel-Aviv

Jamaica The Scientific Research Council of Jamaica, Post Office Box 350, Kingston 6

Kuwait Kuwait Institute for Scientific Research (KISR), Post Office Box 12009, Kuwait City

Libya The Industrial Research Centre: Building Materials Unit, Post Office Box 3633, Tripoli

Malaysia National Institute for Standards and Industrial Research, Batu Tiga, Malaysia

Mexico Institute of Architectural Research, Universidad Nacional Autónoma de Mexico, ENA Ciudad Universitaria, Mexico 20 DF

Singapore Institute of Standards and Industrial Research, 179 River Valley Road, Singapore 6

South Africa National Building Research Institute (NBRI), Post Office Box 395, Pretoria 0001

Sri Lanka Building Research Institute, State Engineering Corporation of Sri Lanka, 99/1 Jawatte Road, Colombo 5

Sudan National Building Research Station, University of Khartoum, Post Office Box 487, Khartoum

Tanzania National Housing and Building Research Unit, Post Office Box 9344, Dar es Salaam

Trinidad The Caribbean Industrial Research Institute (CARIRI), University Post Office, St Augustine

Turkey Building Research Institute, Scientific and Technical Research Council of Turkey, Ataturk Bulvari 243, Kavaklidere, Ankara

USA Building Research Advisory Board, National Research Council, 2101 Constitution Avenue, Washington DC 20418

Zambia National Council for Scientific Research, Post Office Box CH 158, Chelston, Lusaka

113

Plants for arid zones

Introduction

Vegetation in the form of trees, shrubs, creepers and ground covers can, as has already been explained, be effectively used to improve the microclimate of a building in the following ways:

Providing shade—deciduous trees are excellent for shade in summer while allowing sun through during the cold months. Evergreens can be effectively used for shading the building or outdoor areas from the low-lying sun if the right type is selected. Deciduous creepers growing over a pergola or on a wall surface can provide shade for the summer and permit sun to penetrate when it is needed in winter.

Air cooling—moisture from plants can assist in lowering the air temperature by evaporative cooling and the environment adjacent to buildings can be tempered by the use of ground covers and shrubs.

Ventilation—vegetation affects air flow which can be accelerated or directed through buildings by correct and careful planning as long as the behaviour of the flow is predictable. Great care must be taken, however, to ensure that the free flow of cooling breezes is not obstructed.

Shelter—dense planting of evergreen vegetation (preferably in two or three rows) can be used to form windbreaks, provide protection against wind-blown dust and sand, and as screens (both visual and for privacy), as well as for reducing glare.

As vegetation grows easily and often densely in warm-humid zones—the main problem can be to restrict its growth or find trees and shrubs which will not obstruct the flow of breezes—no attempt will be made to provide information here on specific plant types for these areas. In the hot-arid zones, on the other hand, vegetation is extremely sparse and as its beneficial influence on the micro-environment can be enormous, some information on planting in these areas is given.

Hot-arid zones

Plants tend to thrive only where conditions are suitable for their particular species. Many different elements of the environment—water, temperature, light, air movement, soil conditions and so on—and their interaction affect the plants directly and indirectly. Plants dominant in each zone tend to possess inherited characteristics which allow them to flourish in that particular environment. In arid locations there are one of two ways in which plants deal with the problem of surviving drought: either evading it by

staying dormant as seeds ready to shoot up when there is sufficient rain, or by resisting the drought. Plants in this second category have evolved various methods to obtain, store or prevent the loss of water. Some, for instance, have root systems which sprawl laterally, others have deep taproots which search out underground water far below the surface—10 m is not uncommon, and they have been known to go down 30 m and more. Succulents, like the cacti, store water in cells in the stem or leaves while many desert plants have minute leaves—or leaves reduced to spikes—and deciduous behaviour to reduce water loss by transpiration.

The amount of water available to plants is dependent upon soil texture and the proportion of rain-water which penetrates the soil; this is either evaporated or stored as capillary water. Whereas in wet zones the clay soils, with their high moisture-holding capacity, are considered to be the wettest and sandy soils the driest, just the opposite is true in arid areas. As Professor Walter explains in his book, *Ecology of Tropical and Subtropical Vegetation* (see Bibliography), a rainfall of 50 mm will only wet the upper 100 mm of clayey soil, but will penetrate to a depth of 500 mm in sandy soil and even deeper in a stony soil. Evaporation follows and in the clay soil, which soon cracks, the upper 50 mm rapidly dries out with 50 per cent of the water being lost. Although the surface of sandy soil dries in the same way, strands of capillary water are quickly broken and around 90 per cent is retained in the soil. Stony soil shows almost no loss by evaporation and, generally speaking, under uniform climatic conditions, one finds trees growing on this type of soil in arid areas with grass on sandy soils, while the clayey ones remain virtually barren.

Shortage of water and soil textures are not the only environmental problems that plants in hot arid zones have to deal with. Two others, for example, are salt and sandstorms, which can physically damage plants through breakage and by shredding the leaves. Soils in most arid climate zones have a high salt content, as the hot sun and low humidity tend, through evaporation, to concentrate the salts in the upper layers and additional amounts are often added through irrigation, manures and fertilisers. There is furthermore little organic matter in most soils of these regions and where plants are to be grown for shade or as ground covers, peat moss, crushed bark or compost should be added to improve the water-holding capacity amongst other things. Mulch (loose material placed over the soil) can help to reduce soil temperatures and evaporation, and to prevent crusting.

rious forms of dry zone plants: annuals which spring to life when rain does fall (left); the Baobab which
res water in its massive trunk (centre) and thick stemmed succulents (right)

nt types

hough a relatively wide range of vegetation will
ive in desert areas and almost anything can be
wn where there is sufficient water, it must be
nembered that there is not one uniform arid climate
me have winter rains and summer droughts, others
reverse; some have two rainy periods, others only
isodic rains, etc). Each area has its own peculiarities
d differs from the others in one way or another. The
t of plants included here is a general one and not all
them may be suitable for each specific region—local
nditions in a given area may suit some ideally, while
hers may not survive. The average height and
read is given for each plant, but size is also
luenced by both climate and soil conditions, and a
int may be considerably smaller or larger depending
on the local circumstances.

s plants can cost a great deal to grow in the arid
eas, it may be advantageous if they can have a dual
nction; in other words a tree or shrub grown for
ade could be selected from those which bear edible
uit. When plants are being selected for use in
proving the microclimate, other considerations
ust be kept in mind. Robert and Marina Adams, in
eir article, Making the Desert Bloom (see Bibliog-
phy), point out one good example, the hardship that
n be caused by hayfever. People in arid areas are
ten unaccustomed to having flowering trees and
rubs around in any numbers and fairly large-scale
antings of this type can increase pollen levels
nsiderably, causing hayfever among the local
habitants.

rees

cacia farnesiana (sweet acacia)
ciduous tree with deep yellow flowers. Grows to 6 m
height with equal spread. A number of this large

genus (the wattles) are evergreen and various species
(eg A. albida, A. arabica etc) are found in a number of
the major deserts around the world.

Albizia
a genus of deciduous trees and shrubs that is closely
related to the acacias. A. julibrissin (silk tree) is a
hardy and drought resistant tree with low wide-
spreading shape, finely divided fern-like leaves and
pink flowers. Height and spread 6 m or more. A.
lebbek is fast growing; loses leaves for a while in
winter and can look untidy at this stage. Height
around 18 m.

Butea frondosa (flame of the forest)
a slow growing, drought resistant deciduous tree
common throughout India and Burma. Normally a
not particularly attractive medium-size tree with hard
leathery trifoliate leaves. It becomes most attractive
towards the end of winter when it is covered with
orange/red blooms. Height 6–9 m.

Casuarina equisetifolia (Australian pine)
fast growing evergreen tree with silver-grey foliage
which makes a good windbreak particularly in coastal
areas. Height 15 m; spread 10 m.

Ceratonia siliqua (carob bean, St John's bread)
native to the Eastern Mediterranean, this tree does
well in hot, dry climates. Leathery, pinnate, dark
green leaves with yellow and red flowers in summer.
Height 7–12 m; spread 4–7 m.

Chilopsis linearis (desert willow, mimbre)
native to New Mexico and Texas, this deciduous tree
has narrow leaves and slender rather drooping
branches. In spring and summer the tree is covered
with small trumpet-shaped fragrant flowers. Height
from 3–8 m.

115

Cupressus arizonica (cypress)
this tree tolerates drier conditions than other species
of the genus. Pyramidal in form and with grey or
silvery foliage, it is fast growing and much used as a
tall screen or windbreak. Height 10–15 m; spread
5–7 m.

Delonix regia (flamboyant)
a large deciduous tree with spreading, flat-topped
crown. Leaves are large and feathery-looking. Although particularly suited to humid coastal conditions, it does well in hot, dry inland areas which are
frost free. Height 9–12 m; spread up to 9 m.

Eucalyptus
large genus of fast-growing evergreen trees (most of
them from Australia), which will grow well even in
poor soils. Some are grown for shade and shelter (eg
E. camaldulensis: height 10–15 m; spread 5–7 m) and
others as ornamental flowering trees (eg E. torquata).
E. lehmannii, which bears pale green-yellow flowers in
late summer and autumn, is drought and wind
resistant and is useful as a windbreak.

Ficus
a very large genus of trees and shrubs which belong to
the same genus as the common fig but usually bear
inedible fruit. Leaves vary in size and shape and plants
range from trees growing to 30 m, to shrubs only a few
metres high. Care must be taken, as many have
extensive root systems.

Gleditsia (honey locust)
a genus of deciduous trees which are quick growing
and drought resistant, and make good shade trees in
hot-dry areas. They are mostly thorny with lacy, light
green foliage that turns yellow in autumn. G.
triacanthos inermis is a variety that is almost thornless
and is most commonly grown in gardens. Height
16 m; spread 10 m.

Jacaranda mimosaefolia
a deciduous tree with large clusters of mauve-blue
bell-shaped flowers in spring. Does best in summer
rainfall areas. Height and spread 7–14 m.

Melia azedarach (syringa, chinaberry, Texas umbrella
tree)
dense and broad-topped; a good deciduous shade
tree. Lilac flowers in spring are followed by small,
yellow berries. Height and spread 7–10 m.

Morus alba (fruitless mulberry)
grows up to 6 m high and wide and is widely used in
the arid regions of America.

Olea (wild olive)
a genus of slow-growing, drought resistant evergreen
trees which tolerate extreme climatic and soil conditions. O. europaea, for example, is found in a

number of the arid areas. Height and spread about
4–6 m.

Parkinsonia aculeata (Jerusalem thorn)
has sparse foliage with thin, slender branches. Bright
fragrant yellow/green flowers in spring. Height
5–10 m.

Palm trees
come in all shapes and sizes, and can have various uses
in the arid zones. They are roughly divided into two
groups: the pinnate or feathery leaf types and the
palmate or fan leaf types. Only one genus of each
group is described here.

The Phoenix genus with feathery leaves range from
the tall P. dactylifera (date palm) which grows to
around 15 m high with a spread of about 5 m, to P.
roebelinii which is a slow-growing dwarf date palm
1·5–2 m high; spread 1–2 m.
Washingtonia (cotton or fan palm) is a genus with
large, fan-shaped fronds which does well in coastal
areas. Dead leaves droop to form a shaggy 'skirt'
around the trunk unless cut away. W. filifera is thick
stemmed with dull grey-green fronds. Height
10–25 m; spread 3–6 m. W. robusta is slender with a
neat crown of bright green fronds.

Pinus halepensis (Jerusalem or Aleppo pine)
although it is not the most beautiful of pines, this
species is suited to dry conditions and shallow soils.
Height 10–12 m; spread 6–8 m.

Pistacia atlantica
a hardy evergreen tree with attractive foliage, which
does well in rocky soils. Height around 6–10 m.

Populus (poplar cottonwood)
a number of species of this genus are now being grown
in the arid zones for shade or as windbreaks. Care
must be taken as the roots of these quick growing
deciduous trees can cause damage. P. alba (white
poplar) is wide-spreading with leaves that are white-
woolly on their underside. Height 15–20 m.
P. nigra (Lombardy poplar), is tall and columnar with
upward-reaching branches. Is often used as a wind
break.

Salix babylonica (weeping willow)
a graceful deciduous tree with long pendulous
branches which does well in areas where water is
available. Height and spread 10–12 m.

Schinus (pepper tree)
a genus of evergreen trees which tolerates dry
conditions and poor soils. They are fast growing and
make good shade trees. S. terebinthifolius is particularly suited to arid conditions and coastal areas.
Height 6 m; spread up to 9 m. S. molle has attractive
drooping foliage. Care must be taken as root systems

116

hallow and wide-spreading. Height and spread
around 7 m.

Tamarindus indica
a large, spreading tree with dense foliage which does
well in coastal and dry areas. Height 15–18 m; spread
10–12 m.

Terminalia catappa (Indian almond)
a large, quick-growing deciduous tree with horizontally spreading branches which does well as a
windbreak in coastal areas. Height around 15 m;
spread 10 m.

Tipuana tipu (or T. speciosa) (yellow jacaranda, pride
of Bolivia)
a fast-growing evergreen tree with branches growing
at many angles to form flattened crown. Bears bright
yellow flowers in spring and summer. Height 7–9 m;
spread up to 5 m.

Ulmus pumila (Siberian or dwarf elm)
an extremely hardy, bushy deciduous tree which
tolerates dry-hot conditions and can be used as a
windbreak. Dark green serrated leaves turn russet in
autumn. Height up to 6 m; spread up to 2·5 m.

Zizyphus jujuba (Chinese jujube)
deeprooted and salt-tolerant tree well suited to arid
areas. Bears clusters of small yellowish flowers in
spring followed by shiny, reddish-brown datelike
fruits which are edible. Z. spina-christi is also often
used for screening or windbreaks. Height 7–9 m.

small trees/large shrubs

Adenium multiflorum
strange slow-growing deciduous succulent tree or
shrub with thick silvery green or grey stem, often with
swollen reservoir at the base. Broad, semi-succulent,
glossy dark green leaves appear on the fleshy branches
after the clusters of small white to pale pink flowers.
Height 1–4 m; spread up to 1·5 m. A. hongel is found
around the Gulf area and through the Sudan.

Callistemon citrinus (bottlebrush)
and other members of this genus which bear red,
crimson or yellow flower spikes, do well in arid areas.
Height and spread around 3 m or more.

Cassia (buttercup tree)
is genus of fast-growing trees—some are deciduous,
some evergreen—are found in Africa, America and
Australia. Most bear clusters of buttercuplike yellow
flowers. Height and spread from 2–5 m.

Cercidium (Palo verde)
genus of woody plants that have green stems and
twigs which act as the main photosynthetic organs. C.
floridum is a deciduous tree which bears clusters of

bright yellow flowers during spring, followed by tiny
leaves which are shed early leaving a fine tracery of
bluish-green leaf stalks. Height and spread up to 8 m.
C. microphyllum is also deciduous, but branches and
leaves are yellow-green. More compact and spiney
than C. floridum. Height and spread 5–6 m.

Dalea spinosa (smoke tree)
a deciduous tree or shrub with a dense network of
ashy grey branches. Good show of fragrant dark blue
flowers in spring. Height 3–6 m.

Dodonaea viscosa 'Purpurea' (purple hop bush)
evergreen tree or shrub which is often grown as hedge
or windbreak. Has many upright stems covered with
willowlike bronzy-green leaves which turn a rich
purple-red in winter. Height 3–5 m; spread 2–4 m.

Erythrina (coral tree)
a large genus of deciduous trees (eg E. indica) and
shrubs which are drought resistant and grow quickly
in good sandy soil. They are noted for their spec-
tacular clusters of flowers (greenish white, yellow,
orange or red), which they bear in winter and spring
before new leaves appear. Height from 2–12 m or
more; spread 2–10 m.

Hakea
a genus of about 100 species of evergreen trees and
shrubs from Australia. Few of them are cultivated—
all endure poor, dry soils.
H. laurina is a shrub or tree (up to 10 m high) which
grows best in dry, sandy soil. Bears attractive pink or
scarlet flowers. H. multilineata is a shrub or tree
(3–4 m high) with deep red bottlebrush-like flowers.

Ipomoea leptophylla (bush moonflower)
one of the large genus of evergreen and deciduous
twining vines, and a few trees and shrubs, known as
morning glory. This shrub or tree (to 3 m) is beautiful
when in flower (funnel-formed and pink) and is
adapted for very dry places because of its enormous
tuberous roots.

Ligustrum (privet)
a genus of evergreen shrubs and trees which adapt a
semi-deciduous habit in cold winters. L. lucidium is
usually grown as a round-headed tree or tall screen—
height 6–9 m; spread 5–6 m—although there are
varieties that grow to only 3 m high. L. ovalifolium
(green privet) is the hardiest. Height 2·5–5 m; spread
2–4 m.

Maerua
genus of small evergreen trees which are fairly drought
resistant. M. caffra, for example, is slow-growing, has
palmate leaves and bears clusters of small tubular
white flowers in spring. Height around 3 m; spread
2 m.

Melaleuca

a large genus of evergreen, flowering trees and shrubs which carry spikes of flowers similar to those of the bottle-brush. Although fairly drought resistant, they do best when watered regularly. M. armillaris is a fast-growing shrub with a weeping habit which does well as a hedge or windbreak in sandy soil. Height 2·5–4 m; spread 1–2 m.

Myoporum

a genus of fast-growing evergreen trees and shrubs which withstand wind and drought. They have slender leaves and bear small starry, white flowers followed by berries. M. insulare is a dense-growing shrub with bright green succulent leaves and purple berries. Height 2·5–4 m; spread 2·5–5 m.

Olneya tesota (desert ironwood)

a slow-growing, evergreen, spiney shrub-tree found in the driest places of south-west USA. In the spring it is covered with clusters of white or purple flowers. Height 2–6 m.

Photinia serrulata (P. dentata)

evergreen tree with young copper-bronze leaves which become a deep green. Bears white flowers in summer followed by red berries. Height 6–9 m; spread up to 5 m. Often pruned for hedge or shrub.

Pittosporum

a genus of evergreen trees and shrubs which grow well in sandy soil. P. crassifolium, with long, glossy, dark green, oval leaves which are silver-grey on the underside, and clusters of brown flowers in the spring, makes a good windbreak in coastal areas. Height up to 6 m; spread 3–4 m. P. tobira is a shady, ornamental tree with leathery dark green leaves. Height 6–8 m; spread 5 m. Can be pruned for use as a shrub.

Plumeria rubra (frangipani)

var. acutifolia is a deciduous tree/shrub that needs protection from wind and fairly regular watering. Has fleshy branches with long ovate leaves and bears waxy cream-yellow flowers which are very fragrant. Height 2–4 m; spread 1·5–2·5 m.

Prosopis (mesquite)

a genus of evergreen or semi-evergreen shrubs and trees that are outstanding in drought resistance and as windbreaks. P. juliflora is 4–6 m high while P. glandulosa torreyana grows to 10 m high and 12 m wide depending on water supply.

Punica granatum (pomegranate)

deciduous and drought resistant; can be grown as a small tree or fountain-shaped shrub. Trumpet-shaped red flowers in spring are followed by large, round, hard-skinned fruits. Height 5–6 m; spread 4–5 m.

Rhus

a genus of evergreen and deciduous trees and shrubs that are drought resistant and do well in sandy soil. R. lancea (karee) is particularly suited to dry areas. Evergreen with a drooping habit, it has dense, glossy, dark green leaves and bears clusters of tiny white flowers in autumn and winter followed by small yellow-brown fruits. Height 3–9 m; spread 3–7 m. R. ovata (sugar bush) an evergreen shrub growing up to 5 m high, is fairly widely grown in some dry areas.

Sophora

a genus of deciduous and evergreen trees and shrubs that are drought resistant and prefer sandy soil. Foliage is delicate and fernlike, and the plants bear drooping clusters of flowers. S. japonica (pagoda tree) is deciduous, gives light filtered shade and is fairly fast growing. Height 5–10 m; spread 3–6 m.

Tamarix (tamarisk)

a genus of deciduous shrubs and small trees with plumed sprays of flowers in spring and summer. T. aphylla (Athel tree), with bright green foliage and pink flowers, is often used as a windbreak. Height up to 6 m; spread up to 4 m. T. pentandra (salt cedar) bears dense clusters of tiny pink flowers and has downy blue-green foliage. Can be maintained as shrub if cut back. Height 2–5 m; spread 2–4 m.

Tecomella undulata

grows in the driest parts of India and the Gulf area. Evergreen, or nearly so, it is normally a stiff shrub of about 3 m, but can grow into a tree of up to 10 m. The bottom of the trunk is often clear of branches and is topped by a rounded rather open crown. Has narrow grey-green leaves and bears small clusters of large cuplike orange blossoms in spring.

Thevetia nereifolia (yellow oleander)

a large evergreen shrub that grows quickly and thrives in hot areas with mild winters; will also do well in sandy soils in coastal areas. Rounded and dense with long narrow leaves, it bears clusters of yellow flowers. Height around 5 m.

Thespesia populnea (Aden apple, Portia tree)

a quick-growing, drought resistant tree with small light yellow hibiscus-like flowers which turn purple by nightfall when they close. Height 4–6 m.

Yucca

a genus of very hardy succulent type plants with stiffish, long pointed leaves; some are almost stemless shrubs, others grow into large trees with picturesque or grotesque trunks. Y. filamentosa, for example, is a nearly stemless shrub with a rosette of blue-green leaves with long loose fibres along their edges. The flowering stem bears clusters of white flowers and grows around 3 m high.

Shrubs/ground covers/creepers

Acalypha wilkesiana (copperleaf)
bushy, quick-growing evergreen shrub which is hardy and drought resistant, and does well in sandy soils. Leaves bronze-green mottled with red. Height 1–3 m; spread up to 1·5 m.

Atriplex (salt bush)
hardy, drought resistant shrubs with bluish- or silvery-grey leaves; various species are grown in arid areas.

Buddleia
a genus of fast-growing shrubs (some are deciduous, some evergreen), which bear dense sprays of flowers. B. alternifolia is an evergreen with a weeping habit bearing lilac flowers in spring. Height 2–4 m; spread 1–2·5 m. B. davidii (butterfly bush or summer lilac) is deciduous and grows like a weed in the deserts of south-west USA. Height and spread 2·5–4 m.

Caesalpinia gilliesii (bird of paradise)
does well in arid zones and is evergreen or deciduous, depending on winter cold. Has attractive filmy or fernlike dark green leaves on a rather open, angular branch structure. Bears clusters of yellow flowers during summer. Height and spread 2–3 m. C. pulcherrima is also hardy under arid conditions.

Carissa macrocarpa (C. grandiflora) (Natal plum)
an evergreen shrub with dark green glossy foliage and starry jasmine-shaped fragrant flowers followed by smooth-skinned fruits, which resemble plums. Height 2·5–4 m; spread 2–3 m.

Cotoneaster
a large genus of deciduous and evergreen shrubs, many of which may do well in hot-arid zones. Two that have proved to grow well in these areas are: C. pannosus (silverleaf), which is erect growing with small grey leaves on slender, arching branches. Small white flowers in spring are followed by dark red berries. Height and spread 3–4 m. And C. lactea (C. parneyi), which has a graceful arching habit, dark green, rather leathery leaves and brilliant red fruits. Height 2 m; spread 2·5 m.

Duranta repens (D. plumeri) (golden dewdrop)
fast growing evergreen shrub which adopts a deciduous habit in cold winters. Has privet-like leaves and bears trailing sprays of bright blue flowers in spring and summer followed by bunches of golden berries. Height 2–4 m; spread 1·5–3 m.

Elaeagnus pungens (silverberry, oleaster)
a tough, hardy evergreen shrub with clusters of small flowers followed by silver berries, which turn brown and then red. Height and spread 3–4 m.

Euonymus japonicus (spindle tree)
an evergreen shrub often used as a hedge. Lustrous deep green leaves and small pink fruits in autumn. Height and spread 2–3 m.

Euphorbia pulcherrima (poinsettia)
this deciduous shrub likes sun and sandy soil, but needs water, particularly during the growing stage. Bears small flowers supported by large bracts (scarlet, pink or white), which persist through winter. Height and spread 1–3 m.

Genista monosperma (white weeping broom)
var. pendula is a tall decorative shrub with almost leafless weeping branches, which are covered with fragrant white pea-flowers in spring. Will resist drought particularly in summer. Height 2 m; spread 1·5 m.

Hibiscus
a genus of deciduous and evergreen shrubs; species and varieties are available to suit all areas. H. syriacus (rose of Sharon) is a deciduous species which bears bell-shaped flowers (various colours available). Height 2·5–3 m; spread 1–2 m.

Ilex (holly)
a genus of evergreen shrubs with spine-edged leaves and bright berries (usually red). I. altaclarensis 'Wilsoni' is one of the best for arid zones. Height 2–3 m.

Juniperus (juniper)
some species of this genus of evergreen trees and shrubs do well in hot-arid zones if watered regularly. The spreading varieties do best—eg J. chinensis 'Pfitzeriana', which grows to a height of about 1 m with a 2 m spread.

Lantana montevidensis (L. Sellowiana) (purple sage)
low evergreen shrub which makes a good ground cover; is drought resistant and thrives in sandy soil. Flowers are borne profusely throughout most of the year—a variety of colours is available. Height 300 mm; spread 1·5 m.

Larrea divaricata (creosote bush)
very common in the south-west of the USA. Gets its name from the lacquer that covers its leaves and smells strongly of creosote after rain. The shrub branches almost direct from the root collar and although almost leafless, in periods of drought it responds to water with large, shiny, dark-green leaves and small yellow flowers. Height 1–2·5 m.

Lippia citriodora (lemon verbena)
a deciduous shrub with spreading habit which prefers sandy soil. Narrow pointed leaves are bright green; bears sprays of fragrant blue-white flowers during summer. Height 2–2·5 m; spread around 1·5 m.

Myrtus communis (English myrtle)
a hardy evergreen shrub which prefers sandy soil. Small, dark green, glossy leaves and bears white flowers followed by bluish-black berries. Height 2–3 m; spread 1–2 m.

Nereum oleander
which does well in dry conditions is available in many varieties. Leaves are long, deep green—sometimes variegated—and lanceolate, and grow in erect whorls on branched stems. Clusters of single or double flowers, usually white or pink, are borne in summer and autumn. Height and spread 2–4 m.

Phormium tenax (New Zealand flax)
leaves are long sword-shaped and stiffly vertical in a fan pattern. Dull red flowers are borne on long erect spikes. Height and spread 1–2 m; flower stems from 1·5–3 m high.

Pyracantha (firethorn)
a genus of evergreen shrubs with a variety of forms and berry colours. The hardiest are the varieties of P. coccinea, which is generally a bushy round-headed species with height and spread of 2–4 m, although some are low-growing and wide-spreading.

Rosemarinus (Rosemary)
evergreen shrubs from the Mediterranean region. R. officinalis, better known as a herb, is attractive all year with long, narrow, dark green leaves and clusters of lavender-blue flowers. Height 1–1·5 m; spread up to 1 m—semi-dwarf varieties are also available. R. prostratus has a dense trailing habit, not growing much higher than 150–200 mm.

Russelia juncea (coral-bell bush)
a low-growing herbaceous shrub which will stand neglect and drought. Has dainty, grass-like foliage with small, insignificant leaves and bears coral-coloured flowers almost continuously. Height 1–1·5 m.

Simmondsia chinensis (coffee bush, quinine plant)
evergreen shrub with slender branches and thick, succulent leaves. Height 1–2 m.

Tecoma stans (now Stenolobium stans)
evergreen shrub with deciduous habit in cold winter areas which does well in arid zones. Bright yellow flowers are followed in autumn by hanging green seed pods. Height 2–3 m; spread 1–2 m.

Vitex agnus-castus (chaste tree)
a hardy evergreen shrub with upright sprays of lavender-blue flowers and greyish leaves. Height about 3 m.

Shrubs and creepers (or climbers)

Bignonia
these are fast growing creepers, normally evergreen, but lose their leaves in areas with cold winters. They need protection from cold winds. Most of the plants formerly known as bignonias have been reclassified. B. grandiflora (Campsis grandiflora), which bears clusters of orange-red trumpet-shaped flowers in summer, and grows to a length of approximately 4 m, is only one of the species which can be used.

Bougainvillea
a wide selection of these evergreen shrubby climbing plants is available with flower bracts in various colours. They climb vigorously and a single plant can cover a large area. They can be grown against walls and trees or over a pergola. B. glabra, with deep purple bracts, is the hardiest.

Ipomoea learii (blue dawn flower)
a fast-growing, hardy evergreen climber which can become rampant. Has heart-shaped small leaves and bears blue flowers throughout much of the year. Length 3–9 m.

Jasminum (jasmine)
a large genus of evergreen shrubs, many of which have a climbing or semi-climbing habit; several species are grown in the hot-arid zones. J. officinale is a climber with fragrant white flowers and grows to a height of 5 m or more, with a spread of 1·5 m. J. sambac has dark green heart-shaped leaves and white sweet-scented flowers, which are borne throughout the year in frost-free areas. Height 2 m; spread 1 m.

Ficus repens (F. pumila) (creeping fig)
is a rapid climber with small heart-shaped leaves. The branches bear tiny 'suckers' by which the plant clings to supports. Length up to 5 m. There are other species of Ficus which can be used as creepers.

Lonicera (honeysuckle)
a large genus of evergreen and deciduous shrubs with sprawling or semi-climbing habit. Various species can be used; one is L. japonica, a climbing species with a number of varieties bearing yellow, cream, white or pink flowers. Length 6–9 m.

Plumbago capensis (plumbago, leadwort)
a quick-growing, drought resistant evergreen shrub with a semi-climbing, rambling habit. Can be used as a ground cover, with support as a creeper, or as a hedge. Bears bright blue flowers through summer and autumn. Height about 2 m.

Senecio confusus
a quick-growing climbing plant with orange-red flowers which can be grown in the hardest of conditions.

Tecomaria capensis (Cape honeysuckle)
an evergreen semi-climber which can also be used as a ground cover. Orange-red flowers in autumn and winter. Length 2–3 m.

Bibliography

Thunbergia alata (black-eyed Susan)
an effective evergreen climbing plant if supported.
Bears bright orange flowers. Length up to 10 m. T.
grandiflora, with pale-blue or white flowers, is a
strong-growing climber, but tender to frost.

Trachelospermum jasminoides (star jasmine)
evergreen with thick clusters of star-like white
flowers; can be trained as a climber or used as a
sprawling shrub for ground cover. Height and spread
−2 m.

Wisteria
a genus of deciduous climbers covered by flowers in
spring before the leaves appear. W. floribund produces the longest flower clusters. Length up to 10 m.
W. sinensis bears white or mauve flowers and can
grow up to 15 m in length.

Ground covers
There are various ground covers which require less
water and attention than grass. Some have been
included under shrubs and a few more are listed
here.

Asparagus sprengeri
a low-growing perennial herb with light-green,
fernlike leaves. When planted 1·5 m apart they
eventually form a dense ground cover.

Carpobrutus
a genus of prostrate trailing plants which do well even
in pure sand. Have binding roots so can be used on
sandy slopes to prevent erosion etc. Rapidly forms
evergreen ground cover with fleshy leaves and large
flowers (white, yellow or purple).

Polygonum capitatum (pink head knotweed) fast-
growing and dense, and makes a good ground cover.
Has heart-shaped leaves and bears tiny flowers
profusely during spring and summer. Height 100 mm.

Portulaca (rose moss)
a genus of annual and perennial succulents with low,
spreading growth of fleshy foliage which does well as
ground cover in dry, and even poor soil. P. grandiflora
a low-growing with rose-like flowers (white, yellow,
pink, red or orange).

Vinca (periwinkle)
a genus of creeping or erect evergreen plants. V.
major, a trailing large-leafed species with lavender-
blue flowers, does well as a ground cover in dry areas.

Climate and climatic zones

Brown, G. W. Jr. editor. *Desert Biology: special topics
on the physical and biological aspects of arid regions.*
Vol. 1 and Vol. 2. New York: Academic Press, 1968
& 1974. 635 pp & 601 pp. A number of this
collection of essays by various experts are of
interest. For example: Causes, Climates and
Distribution of Deserts, The Biology of Desert
Plants (both Vol. I) and Desert Soils (Vol. 2).

Flohn, H. *Climate and Weather.* London: Weidenfeld
& Nicholson, 1969. 253 pp.
A good broad description of the main climatic
elements—radiation, precipitation and wind—and
the climatic zones.

Geiger, R. *The Climate Near the Ground.* Cambridge,
Mass: Harvard University Press, 1966. 611 pp.
A detailed description of microclimatology—the
climatic conditions within approximately 2 m of the
earth's surface which differs significantly from the
overall climate.

Leopold, A. Starker and The Editors of Life. *The
Desert.* Netherlands: Time-Life International,
1961. 191 pp.
A good general introduction to the hot arid zones of
the world.

Mather, J. R. *Climatology: Fundamentals and Applications.* New York: McGraw-Hill, 1974. 412 pp.
The chapters Basic Climatic Elements, Climate,
Clothing and Human Comfort, as well as Climate
and Architecture are useful, although the latter is
largely based on Olgyay.

Money, D. C. *Climate, Soils and Vegetation.* 2nd
edition. London: University Tutorial Press, 1974.
272 pp.
A very good basic book on climate and climatic
zones.

Nir, D. *The Semi-arid World: man on the fringe of the
deserts.* London: Longman, 1974. 187 pp.
A broad study in regional geography and a useful
introduction to these areas of the world.

Oliver, J. E. *Climate and Man's Environment.* New
York: Wiley, 1973. 517 pp.
The first part of the book, which deals with climate
and the environment, is more detailed than most of
the other books listed here. In the second part

(Climate, Man and Man's Activities) the author deals very broadly with the effect of climate on architecture and cities. A useful appendix, with a detailed explanation of the Mahoney Tables, is included.

Petrov, M. P. *Deserts of the World*. New York: Halsted Press, 1976. 447 pp.
A comprehensive description of the deserts of the world, their specific environmental conditions and an assessment of their natural resources.

Pond, A. W. *The Desert World*. New York: Thomas Nelson, 1962. 342 pp.
A non-technical introduction to desert environments with useful chapters on the climate, weather, plants and people of these areas.

Trewartha, G. T. *An Introduction to Climate*. New York: McGraw-Hill, 1954. 402 pp.
The first part of the book describes the elements of climate in detail, while in the second part the individual elements are synthesised into climatic types and regions.

Walton, K. *The Arid Zones*. London: Hutchinson, 1969. 175 pp.
A useful introduction to the climate and landscape which is not too technical.

Buildings—primitive, vernacular and modern

Al-Azzawi, S. H. Oriental Houses in Iraq, in *Shelter and Society*, edited by Paul Oliver. London: Barrie and Rockliff, 1969. pp 91–102.
A description of the courtyard houses and the way they are lived in. Illustrated with photographs, plans and sections.

Allan, E. *Stone Shelters*. Cambridge, Mass: MIT, 1969. 199 pp.
A study of the people, history, geography and vernacular stone shelters in a small area of southern Italy. An excellent book, very well illustrated.

Andersen, K. B. *African Traditional Architecture: A Study of the Housing and Settlement Patterns of Rural Kenya*.
Nairobi: Oxford University Press, 1977. 239 pp.
A very well illustrated book giving a good idea of the construction materials and methods used in the vernacular buildings of this part of the tropics.

Bahadori, M. N. Passive Cooling Systems in Iranian Architecture. *Scientific America*, Vol. 238, No. 2, February 1978, pp 144–154.
A very interesting article which discusses wind towers, air vents, cisterns and ice makers and is illustrated with a number of drawings and photographs.

Cain, A., Ashfar, F. and Norton, J. Indigenous Building and the Third World. *Architectura Design*, Vol. 45, No. 4, April, 1975, pp 207–224.

Cain, A. et al. Traditional Cooling Systems in the Third World. *The Ecologist*, Vol. 6, No. 2, February 1976, pp 60–64.
Maziara cooling jars and the various ways in which they are used, are described and illustrated.

Cantacuzino, S. and Browne, K. Isfahan. A special issue of *The Architectural Review*, Vol. 159, No 951, May 1976, pp 254–321.
A very attractively presented issue. Of special interest are the descriptions and illustrations of the bazaar and some courtyard houses.

Cantacuzino, S. and Browne, K. The United Arab Emirate. A special issue of *The Architectural Review*, Vol. 161, No. 964, June 1977, pp 325–397
A beautifully illustrated issue on this part of the Middle East. Includes good photographs, drawing and a description of the merchants' houses in the Bastakia district of Dubai with their distinctive courtyards and wind-towers.

Costa, P. and Vicario, E. *Yemen: Land of Builders*. London: Academy Editions, 1978. 176 pp.
A survey of building types and materials of Yemen with four different towns—Zabid, Marakha Sa'dah and San'a—being presented in detail. Illustrated by excellent black and white and colour photographs.

Doumanis, O. B. and Oliver. P. editors. *Shelter i Greece*. Athens: Architecture in Greece Press, 1974 173 pp.
A collection of ten articles covering various aspect of Greek vernacular shelter. Well illustrated with black and white photographs and drawings.

Engel, H. *The Japanese House: a tradition fc contemporary architecture*. Rutland, Vermont Tuttle, 1964. 495 pp.
An excellent book with an interesting chapter o climate in building.

Fathy, H. *Architecture for the Poor: An Experiment Rural Egypt*. Chicago: University of Chicago Press 1973. 346 pp.
The story of an experimental village designed for group of Egyptian peasants using materials avai able locally and appropriate technology. Illustrate by over 100 pages of black and white photograph

Fitch, J. M. *American Building: The Environment Forces that Shape It*. 2nd edition. Boston: Houg ton Mifflin, 1972. 349 pp.
An important study of what has gone wrong ar why, and what can be done about creating a mo

harmonious relationship between buildings and their environment.

Fitch, J. M. and Branch, D. P. Primitive Architecture and Climate. *Scientific America*, Vol. 203, No. 6, December 1960, pp 134–144.
A broad outline of traditional housing in various climatic zones around the world.

Gardi, R. Indigenous African Architecture. New York: Van Nostrand Reinhold, 1973. 249 pp.
This is not a technical book, rather a portfolio of excellent photographs, both black and white and colour, with an accompanying text.

Jackson, P. and Coles, A. Bastakia Wind-tower Houses. *The Architectural Review*, Vol. 158, No. 941, July 1975. pp 51–53.
A short description of the houses illustrated by photographs and drawings.

Oliver, P. editor. *Shelter in Africa*. London: Barrie & Jenkins, 1971. 240 pp.
Sixteen articles on various aspects of vernacular buildings in Africa with examples from hot-dry, warm-wet and intermediate zones.

Parachek, R. E. *Desert Architecture*. Phoenix: Parr of Arizona, 1967. 93 pp.
An illustrated history of the architecture in the Sonora Desert (south-west USA). Soleri's Dome and Earth houses are illustrated.

Rapoport, A. *House Form and Culture*. Engelwood Cliffs, NJ: Prentice-Hall, 1969. 146 pp.
This book considers how houses throughout the world reflect not only the physical conditions of their environments but also the social and cultural. Useful chapters on climate as well as construction, materials and technology as modifying factors.

Rudofsky, B. *Architecture without Architects*. New York: The Museum of Modern Art, 1965. 123 pp.
Hundreds of photographs and short descriptions of indigenous buildings around the world.

Rudofsky, B. *The Prodigious Builders*. London: Secker and Warburg, 1977. 383 pp.
Examples of primitive and vernacular buildings including various forms of underground dwellings and building elements such as grills, screens, shutters, wind-towers etc.

Rodger, A. The Sudanese Heat Trap. *The Ecologist*, Vol. 4, No. 3, March/April 1974, pp 102–106.
The buildings and life-style adapted by the inhabitants of the Sudanese desert, to enable them to survive in this harsh environment, are described.

Williams, C. *Craftsmen of Necessity*. New York: Random House, 1974. 182 pp.

Amongst other things this book contains descriptions, and a number of photographs, of the underground village of Tijia in Southern Tunisia, and the moulded, whitewashed mud 'beehive' dwellings on the north-west plains of Syria.

Climate and design

Aronin, J. E. *Climate and Architecture*. New York: Reinhold, 1953. 304 pp.
Although published over 25 years ago, this book is still useful as an introduction to the demands and phenomena of macro- and microclimate and the response required in the design of buildings.

Building Research Establishment: Overseas Division. *Overseas Building Notes*. Garston, Watford: BRE.
No. 145. *Durability of Materials for Tropical Building*. August 1972.
No. 158. *Building for Comfort*. October 1974.
No. 164. *The Thermal Performance of Concrete Roofs and Reed Shading Panels under Arid Summer Conditions*. October 1975.
No. 176. *Building Materials in the Gulf—their production and use*. October 1977.
No. 177. *Avoiding Faults and Failures in Building*. December 1977.

Danby, Miles. *Grammar of Architectural Design: With Special Reference to the Tropics*. London: Oxford University Press, 1963. 243 pp.
Contains a chapter on climate and design with a number of photographs and diagrams.

Danz, E. *Architecture and the Sun: an international survey of sun protection methods*. London: Thames & Hudson, 1967. 149 pp.
Text in German, English and Spanish. Illustrations: plans, diagrams and photographs.

Design of Low Cost Housing and Community Facilities. Vol. 1: *Climate and house design*. New York: United Nations, 1971.
The main body of the book consists of a detailed explanation of the Mahoney Tables; to illustrate their use examples are given for locations in five different hot climate zones.

Evans, M. Designing in the Tropics. *The Architects' Journal*, Vol. 166, No. 46, 16 November 1977, pp 977–988.
A great deal of useful information is given, much of it in tabular form.

Fry, M. and Drew, J. *Tropical Architecture in the Dry and Humid Zones*. London: Batsford, 1964. 264 pp.
Although some of the information given (eg comparison of labour and material costs) is obviously outdated, this well illustrated book contains a great deal of useful material.

Givoni, B. *Man, Climate and Architecture*. 2nd edition. Barking, Essex: Applied Science, 1976, 473 pp.
A very good technical book covering a wide field from the climatic elements, physiological and sensory responses, building materials and structures, to the mechanisms of ventilation. Chapter 17, which discusses the principles of design and selection of materials to adapt buildings to various hot climate zones, is particularly useful.

Golany, G. editor. *Urban Planning for Arid Zones: American experience and directions*. New York: Wiley, 1978. 245 pp.
A collection of articles of varying interest divided into five sections, each related to a different aspect of urban planning. Those which describe and evaluate the physical factors such as climate, soil etc, are useful anywhere, while those covering social and economic issues of the American south-west are much less so.

Harkness, E. L. and Mehta, M. L. *Solar Radiation Control in Buildings*. Barking, Essex: Applied Science Publishers, 1978. 285 pp.
This book examines solar geometry, the calculation of solar radiation heat loads, orientation, form, fenestration and the effectiveness of sunscreens, amongst other things.

Koenigsberger, O. H. *et al*. *Manual of Tropical Housing and Building*. Part 1: *Climatic Design*. London: Longman, 1973. 320 pp.
A good textbook for students and reference work for designers and others involved in the building process. Covers not only climatic elements, zones and thermal comfort as well as the principles of design, but also descriptions and recommendations for shelters in various zones. Also included are details of the Mahoney Tables and solar charts (as well as a shadow angle protractor) for latitudes 0–44° N and S.

Koenigsberger, O. and Lynn, R. *Roofs in the Warm Humid Tropics*. Architectural Association Paper No. 1. London: Lund Humphries, 1965. 56 pp.
An evaluation of and comparison between different roofing materials and methods of construction to assist designers in making a rational choice.

Kukreja, C. P. *Tropical Architecture*. New Delhi: Tata McGraw-Hill, 1978. 133 pp.
The book deals with both theoretical and practical aspects of designing buildings in the tropics. The effects of sun, wind, landscaping, local building materials, aesthetic considerations and construction techniques are analysed. The coverage has special relevance to regions in South-East Asia and the Middle East.

Lee, K. *Encyclopaedia of Energy-efficient Building Design: 391 practical case studies*. Vols 1 and 2. Boston: Environmental Design and Research Centre, 1977. 1023 pp.
An examination of recent projects utilising energy conscious design principles and showing an awareness of the importance of climatic conditions. Included in the buildings and projects illustrated are, for example, a number of underground structures as well as cluster designs for both hot-arid and hot-humid climates.

Lippsmeier, G. *Building in the Tropics*. Munich: Callwey, 1969. 282 pp.
Produced bilingually (German and English) this compendium of information on building in tropical countries lays particular emphasis upon the problems of developing states.

McHenry, P. G. Jr. *Adobe: build it yourself*. Tucson: University of Arizona Press, 1973. 157 pp.
A thorough book on many aspects of adobe construction.

Merrilees, D. and Loveday, E. *Pole Building Construction*. Enlarged edition. Charlotte, VI: Garden Way, 1975. 102 pp.
Although this book does not exploit fully the forms and details made possible by this form of construction, and tends to stick to standard methods, it does outline the basic principles and techniques involved.

Oakley, D. *Tropical Houses: a guide to their design*. London: Batsford, 1961. 272 pp.
Although this book was published almost 20 years ago, it contains a great deal of relevant and useful information.

Olgyay, V. *Design with Climate: bioclimatic approach to architectural regionalism*. Princeton, NJ: Princeton University Press, 1963. 190 pp.
An excellent book covering the theory of climatic design which has become almost a classic in this field.

Olgyay V. and Olgyay A. *Solar Control and Shading Devices*. Princeton, NJ: Princeton University Press, 1957 (new edition: 1976). 202 pp.
The theory of solar control with numerous examples of various types of shading devices.

Saini, B. S. *Architecture in Tropical Australia*. Architectural Association Paper No. 6. New York: George Wittenborn, 1970. 67 pp.
The hot climate zones of Australia are described and the responses required to produce buildings which are physiologically and psychologically comfortable in each area are discussed.

Saini, B. S. *Building Environment: an illustrated analysis of problems in hot dry lands.* Sydney: Angus and Robertson, 1973. 148 pp.
A comprehensive examination of the problems confronting building designers in the arid zones. Solutions are illustrated by many examples of completed buildings.

Van Straaten, J. F. *Thermal Performance of Buildings.* Amsterdam: Elsevier, 1967. 311 pp.
A technical book with detailed information on the principles of heat transfer, thermal and physiological requirements, insulation and ventilation.

Wakeling, T. R. M. and Head, J. M. Geotechnics in a hot desert environment. *Middle East Construction,* Vol. 2, No. 1, Nov 1977, pp 111–114.

Wright, D. *Natural Solar Architecture: a passive primer.* Florence, KY: Van Nostrand Reinhold, 1978. 256 pp.
A comprehensive book explaining how to let nature do most of the work.

Hazards

Afshar, F. *et al.* Mobilising Indigenous Resources for Earthquake Construction. *Housing Science,* Vol. 2, No. 4, 1978, pp 335–350.
Proposals for a methodology for the upgrading of village building to better withstand earthquakes. Illustrated by a number of photographs and line drawings.

Building Research Establishment: Overseas Division. Overseas Building Notes. Garston, Watford: BRE. No. 143. *Building in Earthquake Areas.* April 1972. No. 170. *Termites and Tropical Building.* October 1976.

Dowrick, D. J. *Earthquake Resistant Design: a manual for engineers and architects.* London: Wiley, 1977. 374 pp.
A most useful book which explains all the major factors relating to the design of structures in any material in order to minimise damage from earthquakes. Detailed consideration is given to soils, foundations, superstructure and non-structural elements, and also to the interaction between them.

Golde, R. H. editor. *Lightning.* Vol. 1: *Physics of Lightning* and Vol. 2: *Lightning Protection.* London: Academic Press, 1977. 849 pp.
The first volume is very technical and does not contain much of practical use for the designer. In Vol. 2, however, there are valuable chapters, particularly 17 The Lightning Conductor, 18 Lightning Earths, and 19 Protection of Structures.

Houghton, E. L. and Carruthers, N. B. *Wind Forces on Buildings and Structures: an introduction.* London: Edward Arnold, 1976. 243 pp.
A rather technical book intended for students of civil engineering and practising engineers, but should be read by architects planning buildings in zones where wind can be a hazard.

Marshall, J. L. *Lightning Protection.* New York: Wiley, 1973. 190 pp.
A thorough book describing lightning damage and the precautions that can be taken.

McDowell, B. Earthquake in Guatemala. *National Geographic,* Vol. 149, No. 6, June 1976, pp 810–829.
The story of one of the worst disasters ever to hit the Western Hemisphere, with a number of colour photographs.

Report of the Committee on the Protection of Building Timbers in South Africa against Termites, Wood-boring Beetles and Fungi. Pretoria: National Building Research Institute, 1950. 209 pp.
Detailed information on the various types of termites etc and the recommended practice for proofing new buildings against them.

United Nations: Office of the Disaster Relief Co-ordinator. *Disaster Prevention and Mitigation: A Compendium of Current Knowledge.*
Vol. 1: *Volcanological Aspects.* Geneva: United Nations, 1976, 38 pp.
Vol. 2: *Hydrological Aspects.* Geneva: United Nations, 1976.
Vol. 3: *Seismological Aspects.* New York: United Nations, 1978. 127 pp.
Vol. 4: *Meteorological Aspects.* New York: United Nations, 1978. 96 pp.
Vol. 5: *Land Use Aspects.* New York: United Nations, 1978. 69 pp.
Vol. 6: *Engineering Aspects.* (In preparation.)
Vol. 12: *Preparedness Aspects.* (In preparation.)

United Nations: Office of the Disaster Relief Coordinator. *Guidelines for Disaster Prevention.*
Vols 1–3. Geneva: United Nations, 1976.
Vol. 1: *Pre-disaster Physical Planning of Human Settlements.* 93 pp.
Vol. 2: *Building Measures for Minimising the Impact of Disasters.* 59 pp.
Vol. 3: *Management of Settlements.* 84 pp.

United Nations: Department of Economic and Social Affairs. *Low-cost Construction Resistant to Earthquakes and Hurricanes.* New York: United Nations, 1975. 205 pp.

Wiegel, R. L. editor. *Earthquake Engineering.* Engelwood Cliffs, NJ: Prentice-Hall, 1970. 518 pp.
A very technical book intended mainly for en-

gineers but it contains useful information for architects, particularly the descriptions of structural damage during various earthquakes in the USA (Chapter 9), and of soil problems (Chapter 10).

Yanev, P. *Peace of Mind in Earthquake Country*. San Francisco: Chronicle Books, 1974. 304 pp.
The book not only describes the phenomena, but also what to do about them—how to evaluate sites and buildings, and how to design for this hazard.

Underground buildings

Brock, T. The Plowboy Interview: Andy Davis. *The Mother Earth News*, No. 46, July/August 1977, pp 18–28.
Davis describes the underground home he built for himself. Illustrated with a number of colour photographs and a few diagrams.

Fairhurst, C. and Bligh, T. *Earth Sheltered Housing Design*. Minneapolis, Minn: The Under Ground Space Centre, University of Minnesota, 1978.
A collection of symposium papers which covers the subject in great detail. A good bibliography is included.

Golany, G. Energy-Free Cooling Systems for Houses in Deserts. In *Innovations for Future Cities* edited by Gideon Golany. New York: Praeger, 1976, pp 246–262.
A short discussion on the use of subterranean dwellings in arid climates and ways of planning for ventilation as well as humidification.

Marcovitch, S. J. Autonomous living in the Ouroboros House. *Popular Science*, Vol. 207, No. 6, December 1975, pp 80–82 and III.
Description and illustrations of the semi-underground experimental house at the University of Minnesota.

Marcovich, S. J. Buried Bookstore: saves energy, saves space, saves the view. *Popular Science*, Vol. 211, No. 3, Sept 1977, pp 96–97.

Moore, K. Coober Pedy: Opal Capital of Australia's Outback. *National Geographic*, Vol. 150, No. 4, October 1976, pp 561–571.
The underground houses of this community are described and illustrated.

Smay, V. E. Underground houses: low fuel bills, low maintenance, privacy, security. *Popular Science*, Vol. 210, No. 4, April 1977, pp 85–89 and 155.
A number of examples of underground houses in America are described and illustrated.

Wells, M. Underground Architecture. *The CoEvolution Quarterly*, No 11, Fall 1976, pp 85–92.
General information on building underground including a number of diagrammatic sketches and photographs of Wells' own underground office.

Wells, M. *Underground Design*. Cherry Hills, NJ: Malcolm Wells, 1977. 87 pp.
A short book prepared in response to the large number of enquiries the author received after publication of the above-mentioned article.

Solar energy and water

Anderson, B. *Solar Energy: fundamentals in building design*. New York: McGraw-Hill, 1977. 374 pp.
A well-illustrated book covering the basics of heat theory, insolation, solar angles and shading etc, as well as practical information on designing buildings to save energy and utilise the available solar radiation.

Cawood, W. N. and Billingham, P. A. *Introductory Guide to Solar Energy and Solar Water Heaters*. Pretoria: National Building Research Institute of the CSIR, 1976. 39 pp.
Basic introduction to water heating using solar energy: how to install a system and how to construct a heater illustrated step by step with a series of photographs.

Chinnery, D. N. W. *Solar Water Heating in South Africa*. Pretoria: National Building Research Institute of the CSIR, 1971. 79 pp.
A detailed publication on the construction and installation of flat-plate collectors.

Daniels, F. *Direct Use of the Sun's Energy*. New York: Ballentine, 1974. 271 pp.
Contains useful chapters on solar radiation, collectors thereof, heating water and distillation.

The Editors of Sunset Books. *Homeowner's Guide to Solar Heating*. Menlo Park, California: Lane Publishing, 1978. 96 pp.
The book describes the use of solar energy to heat homes in temperate areas, but many of the basic concepts of designing with climate are simply explained with numerous diagrams.

Milne, M. *Residential Water Conservation*. Davis, California: California Water Resources Centre, 1975. 468 pp.
Includes amongst other things information on dozens of home devices to save water and an extensive annotated bibliography.

Ortega, A. *et al. The Ecol Operation ecology + building + common sense*. Revised edition. Montreal: Minimum Cost Housing Group, McGill University, 1975. 128 pp.

Price, T. Low-technology Solar Homes that work with nature. *Popular Science*, Vol. 209, No. 6, December 1976, pp 95–98 and 143.
A number of interesting houses, most of them built of adobe, are described. Well illustrated with drawings and photographs.

Rybczynski W. and Ortega, A. *et al. Stop the Five Gallon Flush! A survey of alternative waste disposal systems.*
Montreal: Minimum Cost Housing Group, McGill University, 1973. 68 pp.

Steadman, P. *Energy, Environment and Building.* Cambridge: Cambridge University Press, 1975. 287 pp.
Contains useful chapters on energy conservation measures in buildings, solar energy and water collection and conservation.

Stein, R. G. *Architecture and Energy: Conserving Energy Through Design.* Garden City, NY: Doubleday, 1977. 322 pp.
A non-technical, well-documented book with many actual examples.

Stoner, C. H. editor. *Goodbye to the Flush Toilet.* Emmanus, PA: Rodale Books, 1977. 285 pp.
Overall view of composting privies and toilets, and greywater recycling.

Szokolay, S. V. *Solar Energy and Building.* 2nd edition. London: The Architectural Press, 1977. 192 pp.
A broad survey of solar energy, its collection and use. The core of the book contains an illustrated technical review of a number of 'solar houses' from around the world, and the vast expansion in solar installation that has taken place in recent years.

Vale, B. and R. *The Autonomous House: design and planning for self-sufficiency.* London: Thames & Hudson, 1975. 224 pp.
Solar energy, recycling of waste, water collection and greywater recycling are discussed among other things.

Van der Ryn, S. *The Toilet Papers.* Santa Barbara, California: Capra Press, 1978. 127 pp.
A useful and well illustrated book on dry toilets and greywater systems.

Van Dresser, P. *Homegrown Sundwellings.* Santa Fe, NM: The Lightning Tree, 1977. 135 pp.
Some of Van Dresser's most recent explorations of the possibilities inherent in simple solar architecture constructed from local materials.

Planting

Adams, R. and M. Making the Desert Bloom. *The Architectural Review*, Vol. 161, No. 964, June 1977, pp 353–358.

Adams, R. and M. and Willens, A. and A. *Dry Lands: man and plants.* London: The Architectural Press, 1978. 152 pp.
A most useful book describing the dry lands of the world, their ecology and vegetation. Of particular value to those involved in environmental planning, large-scale developments and agriculture.

Coghlan, R. *Landscape Gardening in the Tropics.* London: Hart-Davis, MacGibbon, 1975. 174 pp.
Includes lists of plants suitable for use in dry soils and as windbreaks.

Clouston, B. *Landscape Design with Plants.* London: Heinemann, 1977.
Included in the three sections of chapters written by 24 authors are two chapters and numerous illustrations giving an introduction to plants and design in the tropics.

The Editors of Sunset Magazine and Sunset Books. *Desert Gardening.* Menlo Park, California: Lane Books, 1967. 96 pp.
A useful background to plant types and landscaping ideas, particularly for south-west USA, with many black and white photographs.

Evenari, M., Shanan, L. and Tadmor, N. *The Negev: the challenge of a desert.* Cambridge, Mass: Harvard University Press, 1971. 345 pp.
A detailed study of the desert, agricultural techniques and life with a minimum of water.

Jennings, C. *Drought Gardening.* Boring, OR: Charles Jennings, 1977. 48 pp.
This booklet presents tips on coping with little water, as well as an over-all strategy for scaling down the garden to suit dry conditions.

Menninger, E. A. *Flowering Trees of the World for Tropics and Warm Climates.* New York: Hearthside Press, 1962. 336 pp.
Descriptions of 500 trees with many colour photographs and some drawings.

Robinette, G. O. *Plants, People and Environmental Quality.* Washington: US Dept. of Interior, National Park Service, 1972. 140 pp.
A useful book for designers, explaining how plants can be used to dampen sound and control sun, wind, rain and temperature, amongst other things.

Van-Ollenbach, A. W. *A Planting Guide to the Middle East.* London: The Architectural Press, 1978. 154 pp.
Descriptions of trees, shrubs and other plants suitable for this area, illustrated by 150 line

drawings. Includes a number of useful appendices providing additional information in tabular form.

Walter, H. *Ecology of Tropical and Subtropical Vegetation.* Edinburgh: Oliver & Boyd, 1971. 539 pp.
Describes in detail the vegetation of not only the various arid regions of the world, but also that of the humid tropics and the savannahs.

Acknowledgements

I would like to thank Charles Swanepoel for preparing the line illustrations.
The photographs are taken from the following sources:
The Architectural Press: pp. 8, 32, 42, 48 (top and below left), 51 (top centre, left, bottom left, bottom right), 56 (left), 62, 86
Building Research Establishment: p. 62
Japanese Government: p. 43
Allan Konya: pp. 45 (above), 49, 51 (top left and right)
Mark Konya: p. 90
C. Meintjies: p. 23
National Tourist Organisation of Greece: pp. 24, 93
Thomas and Poul Pedersen: p. 45 (below right)
Paul Popper Ltd: p. 32
Pretoria News: p. 20
Rhodesian Ministry of Information: p. 21
Satour: p. 115 (left, centre and right)
Constance Stuart Photography: pp. 45 (below left), 94, 95

ndex